DeFunkMe

THE BASIX

SIX ESSENTIALS TO BEAT STRESS, DEPRESSION & ANXIETY

Ian Schell

Publishing information

Legal Disclaimer

This book is no substitute for the medical advice of suitably qualified physicians. The reader should regularly consult the appropriately qualified physicians regarding any matters of health. The author has made every reasonable effort to ensure the information and opinions in this book are correct at the time of publishing. The author and publisher hereby disclaim any liability regarding adverse effects resulting from any action taken based on any information in this book. The author advocates self-education of the reader. The reader must thoroughly research any advice, diagnosis, prescriptions, and treatments before deciding what action to take for themselves.

Edited by Rebecca Wylie of Sage Written Word

Cover Design by VOVO Designs (via 99 Designs)

A copy of this publication can be found in the National Library of Australia

National Library of Australia Cataloguing-in-Publication entry:

Creator: Schell, Ian, Author

Title: DeFunkMe: The Basix / Ian Schell

ISBN 978-0-6480464-0-0 (Paperback)

ISBN 978-0-6480464-1-7 (Ebook - Epub)

ISBN 978-0-6480464-2-4 (Ebook – Kindle/Mobi)

ISBN 978-0-6480464-3-1 (Audiobook – Audible)

Subjects: Stress (Psychology)--Prevention. Stress management. Depression, Mental--Prevention. Anxiety--Prevention.

First Publication, 2017

All enquiries and correspondence to:

Ian Francis Schell

Email: ian@defunkme.com

www.defunkme.com

Dedication

I want to thank my lovely wife, Margret, my rock, the one who stuck it out when so many others would have bailed. Thank you for putting me onto '30 Days of Genius' which featured James Altucher, author of *Choose Yourself!*, who suggests the '10 ideas daily practice', which gave me the idea to write this book. You sowed the first seed which grew into this book.

Thank you to the rest of my family who helped me get through all of this. Especially my Dad, who has always been there for me when I needed him the most.

Thank you to the wonderful staff at Palladium Private™ that showed me the way.

My biggest wish is that my children learn this information and apply it to their lives. I think that the information in this book should be taught in schools—minus my colourful language, of course.

> *"… it has had a great impact on me, and I can relate so much better with members of my family who struggle with ups and downs. I love the work you have done, your honesty and respect for the individual's ability to 'cope' with some of life's traumas. Great read."*
> Julie Townrow – Author

Before we begin

In October 2014, I knew something was seriously wrong. I wasn't quite suicidal, but I started having thoughts of ending it all. Any thought remotely like that is a bloody good indication that it is time to seek help. If you have thoughts of suicide, please seek help immediately.

Even if you feel like you have no-one in your life that cares about you, I am willing to bet that there is—and more than you probably know. Those people left behind will grieve, who in turn affect a handful of their friends and family with their grief. What sort of example does suicide set for those people left behind, particularly young people who can't quite grasp what is going on yet?

Even though you may not feel like it now, life is such a gift. No matter how bad life is or what has been done, life can be rebuilt—bigger and better than ever, if you want it to be.

Be kind to yourself! I believe that everyone, at some point in their life, goes through some form of depression or feeling of being trapped. It is OK to not be OK. Swallow your pride and go get help when you're down, because pride doesn't count for shit. Remember this saying:

This too shall pass.

Who knows, when you get through it, you might be able to help someone else in a similar situation.

If you or a loved one feels suicidal:
- **Call emergency services immediately.** In Australia it's 000, in New Zealand it's 111, in the US it's 911. Don't think that it's not an emergency—there's a life on the line. Call them.
- Google it! Google 'I need help', and even more importantly, follow through to GET HELP. There is a sea of organisations and people out there who want to help you if you let them.
- Go to your nearest hospital or doctor.

What else can you do?
- Quiet the mind. When in turmoil or distress, the mind is generally in overdrive, banging around all the worst possible thoughts imaginable. You need to quiet that down.
- Trust that life will get better! Focusing on the bad will only make you feel worse; try to look for the 'silver linings', any positive possibilities that can come from a shitty situation. There are positives in EVERY situation—you just may not be able to see them yet.
- Have a cry and a good sleep. Crying is healthy, it releases tension, and can help you feel better.
- Talk to your friends and family. 'A problem shared is a problem halved'.
- Listen to soothing music.
- Go for a brisk walk. Get the endorphins going (the natural happy drugs your body produces with exercise). It can be 5 minutes or 30 minutes—just get moving, get the blood pumping.
- Focus on your breathing. Nice big deep breaths. Fill your

lungs and imagine your pain or stress flowing out with every breath. Keep focusing on your breath. If your thoughts run away again, return your focus to your breath. See the section in this book on meditation for more.

Avoid:
- Drugs, alcohol and stimulants. They may take the pain or anguish away for now, but ultimately, the pain will be back and even worse with the comedown or hangover.
- Sugars and carbs. Sugars are depressants. Carbs are treated similarly to sugar. Eat fresh natural foods.
- Fast foods. Gumming up your system with shit food won't make you feel any better.
- Being alone.

The Highlight Reel: Choose to feel better in an instant

One of my favourite methods to feel better in no time is to review the 'highlight reel'. Find a nice quiet spot where you are not likely to be interrupted and think about the 'highlight reel' of your life.

What events in your life have brought you the most joy?

It might have been your first kiss, an amazing love-making session, a place that you have been, experiences you have had, adventures that you have been on, laughing fits where you lost your shit, etc. Think about those moments and re-live them; experience all of the joy and positive emotions once again.

Cherish the memories and feel gratitude for such great times.

Any time that you feel a bit down, quickly remember the top one or two of these highlights and focus intensely on the joy and memory of that moment. Do this for long enough to shift the focus away from what it is that got you down.

And rest assured that you will have more moments like that if you just ride out the tough times. Life is a rollercoaster full of ups and downs—tolerate the downs and look forward to the ups.

Table of Contents

DeFunkMe: The Basix

A thank you gift

Thank you for buying *DeFunkMe: The Basix*.

I am a realist and statistics show that a majority of you won't finish this book. It's just the way it is with most books. We all have good intentions of buying and reading books, but sometimes life just gets in the way, and that is OK.

I feel that the information in this book is too important to miss out on. This is the one book that I wish that I had when I was a teenager.

Just for buying my book, I have a gift for you! I have condensed all of the essential information in this book into an infographic poster. The message is simplified, but the content is powerful—if you apply it! Get your free gift by going to:

defunkme.com/gift

Can I ask a favour in return? Please leave a brief but HONEST review of this book wherever you purchased it.

As an author, our success hinges on purchases and reviews. The more popular this book, the wider I can spread this message to help more people.

Email any feedback, comments, suggestions or questions you may have to: ian@defunkme.com.

Thank you and much love,
Ian Schell

Introduction

On my 21st birthday I tried to commit suicide. Obviously, I fucked that up because I'm still here.

Again in 2014, I hit rock bottom. On paper I had it all—a lovely wife, renovated house, good job and pay, two kids, two cars, two cats. Yet here I was, severely depressed and suicidal. Maybe it was the cats, I don't know.

Now, as of April 2017, I am the happiest and healthiest I have ever been. I look back on my experience in 2014 as the best thing that has ever happened to me. Why? How can going through massive depression be the best thing that has ever happened to me? Because I got good help, new information and practical life tools that have turned my life around. And now, I am on a mission to help others improve their lives.

I very rarely have 'blue' days. I have my own business and am building a second. I am happy with my weight. I have rediscovered my love of learning and personal growth. I have found my zest for life. I am happy with my life. That is all thanks to my depression, my journey and the great help and support that I received.

I am forever grateful for the darkness because now I can appreciate the light.

I write these things to illustrate that massive change is possible.

How did this change happen?

- I made the decision to change.
- I found a facility that dealt with depression naturally, as I didn't want to take any more drugs or medications—they just weren't working as nothing really changed long-term.
- I acquired new information and techniques to change my beliefs and thinking.
- I implemented a new way of eating via a mixture of Paleo and Low Carb High Fat (LCHF) meals.
- Regular exercise became routine.
- Meditation and mindfulness practices.
- Journey therapy.
- Life coaching.

It wasn't easy or cheap.

My hope in writing this book is to pass on the information that I have learned, and that I have found effective in my life. When I first started writing, I was solely concentrating on helping others to overcome depression, anxiety and stress. For some reason this just wasn't sitting quite right with me, I think for a couple of reasons:

1. I didn't want to be pigeon-holed into dealing with just depression or anxiety.
2. A LOT of the information in this book is applicable to every person on the planet, as we all have areas of our lives where we may feel like we are in a funk.

My belief is that everyone wants to live a better life. If I can help just one person improve their life, I will have made a real difference in this world and that would be pretty special to me.

With the information in this book, there is no guarantee of fixing anything. However, I am 100% confident that the information and techniques in this book will greatly improve your life, but only if you choose to apply what you learn.

Nobody else can do it for you. If YOU want change in your life, it is YOU who needs to make that change happen.

All the best information in the world cannot help you if YOU are not willing and committed to change.

I do wish you the best life possible in every aspect.

Change is not easy, but it's worth it. You are worth it!

Here's something that my life coach taught me that I would like to share with you.

> *"Life is like a rubber band. Sometimes we are stretched, sometimes we are pulled in directions we don't want to go. When we are pulled down the hardest and we let go, we can fly the highest."*

DeFunkMe: The Basix

My Journey

This expanded version of my introduction is rather long; it is the story behind my depression and change. You can quite safely skip to the next chapter, but it does help explain a few things later in the book. I think this is an interesting story, but I would because it's mine.

From the beginning

My name is Ian Schell and I was born in Northam Hospital on the 28th of August 1979, the first and only child of Mark and Cherie Schell. Not long after I was born, my parents separated and divorced. I lived with mum for the first seven years of my life. We moved a lot, which meant it was difficult to make and keep friends.

In those first seven years, I remember being shuttled back and forth between my parents. This set up a rather upsetting mental pattern for me as a young child. When I was with Mum, I cried to be with Dad. When I was with Dad, I cried to be with Mum, especially after changing parents. I remember many nights crying myself to sleep, wishing for the other parent.

It wasn't all bad, as I have many fond memories of my parents. I am grateful I had them both and that they loved me, wanted me and treated me well. Even so, I would have given anything to have Mum and Dad together and maybe a brother or sister or two.

Early school years

When I was seven, I clearly remember my mum sitting me down with a serious look on her face. She asked, "Do you want to go and live with your father?" At the time, I had no idea of the magnitude of the choice I had to make. Dad and my grandfather, 'Pa', lived on the farm in Goomalling. I had lived with Mum all of my life, but I longed to live with Dad and missed him dearly. I said yes, and the decision was made.

Mum packed me up and I went to live with Dad on the farm and I started Grade 3 at Goomalling Primary School. I loved living on the farm with Dad and Pa. I was rarely bored, with a motorbike, go-kart, and many afternoons hanging out with Pa, who taught me all sorts of cool shit like how to use his computer, shooting a gun and showing me how things worked.

High school

After primary school, Dad sent me off to board at Swanleigh whilst I attended Governor Stirling Senior High School, or 'Govo' as we used to call it (pronounced guh-voe). Boarding at Swanleigh was possibly the worst period of my life. The culture there was very negative and if you weren't one of the cool kids, you were a nobody. Bullying was rife and the Year 12's ruled the roost.

Being six foot and weighing one hundred kilograms in Year 8, I was bigger and heavier than most of the Year 12's, meaning I stood out with a target on my back. The older students targeted me for lots of bullying, I copped many beatings.

On several occasions, when dad had taken me out for the school holidays or weekends, I pleaded with him in tears not to take me back. I just didn't want to be there—I hated it.

The first two years at Swanleigh were unpleasant, to say the least. Then, the old director resigned, and his replacement slowly turned the place on its head. Over the course of a few months, he managed to stop most of the bullying. There were serious disciplinary repercussions for hitting someone else. Unfortunately, he couldn't do anything for the culture and it remained a particularly negative and sarcastic place.

Despite the bullying, it wasn't all bad. There were fun events, activities, outings, sports and many great memories were made. However, if there was just one period of my life that I could magically go back and change, I would have gone to high school in Northam. But hey, who knows, that could have been even worse, but at least I would have been with Dad and Pa. I missed them terribly while at Swanleigh.

Tertiary studies

After graduating high school, Dad wanted me to do further studies in something—anything. He was insistent on getting some form of qualification under my belt. Thanks to a bad relationship with an English teacher, a university degree was out of the question, so it was either a diploma at TAFE or get an apprenticeship in a manual trade. I enjoyed tech drawing and was good at maths and physics, so I chose mechanical engineering at TAFE which would lead me to become a draftsman. I didn't really know what to do, and this seemed like the best fit.

A major marker in my life happened around the middle of 1998. I needed a computer to do my assignments and learn CAD for TAFE, so Mum and Dad went halves in a relatively expensive computer. I can't remember the specs on it, but it had Windows 98 and an inbuilt modem so I could get on the internet.

Then I discovered Yahoo Chat. I was a bit of a loner and always searching for new connections with people. Chat opened up my world.

Kristykins

One night I was knocking around in a Californian chat room just making idle chitchat with the 'locals'. A new girl with the handle 'Kristykins' popped into the room. I struck up a conversation in the main chat room with her. It's hard to describe, but we had an instant connection. Very soon we changed from the chat room to a private message session. That first night we chatted for hours. We LOL'd so hard, often upgrading to LMAO's. We 'got' each other in every way. The next night I eagerly awaited her arrival in the same chat room and BAM there she was. It was on again! You bloody beauty. This went on most nights. Back then it was almost unheard of having internet relationships, but safe to say; I fell in love with an American girl I had never physically met.

After about three months of regular chatting online, Kristy and

I graduated to talking on the phone. It was possibly one of the most nerve-racking experiences I've ever had, but it was so good to hear her voice for the first time. It was a bit awkward, especially with a slight time lag caused by the international calling distance, but we got used to it and talked for many hours. Around the same time, we exchanged photos and luckily, we both liked what we saw.

The Goal

Two years at TAFE saw me graduate at the end of 1998 with an advanced diploma in mechanical engineering and I landed a job almost immediately as a draftsman for a small, but versatile, engineering company.

Early in 1999 I decided that I wanted to meet Kristy, and she was equally excited about the idea, so I set a goal to fly over to America at the end of 1999. I found a second job as a doorman (bouncer) and lived off one income whilst saving the other for the trip.

Very quickly I had saved enough to purchase the return flights. There was no turning back. The rest of the year was spent working two jobs, saving like mad, chatting and phoning with Kristy. Most of my high school friendships suffered through this period because I was a hermit on a mission. We had planned a massive road trip to see the west coast of the USA, and I managed to save over ten thousand dollars spending money in that year.

I chose to fly out mid-December 1999, so that we could spend Christmas together and then New Year in Vegas—can you imagine? Turn of the millennium in Vegas!

One afternoon, a couple of weeks before departure, I received a tearful phone call from Kristy. She had fallen ill. I can't remember what the problem was, but she had to have an operation. She couldn't afford to pay for the operation, but her father could, and one of the conditions of him paying was that she had to move back home to live with him.

The trip was off. She wanted to wait until she had recovered to do our big road-trip as planned. I was devastated, completely and utterly. I cried for days—plenty of manly sobbing ensued. We still chatted and spoke on the phone, but because of the move, the operation and her father, it wasn't very often. I cancelled all the bookings for the road trip and managed to get the flights put on hold so I could still use them later.

I think this period was my first taste of true depression. Christmas came and went, and I was utterly miserable. On Boxing Day morning, Christmas night in the US, Kristy and I spoke and I distinctly remember getting off the phone and thinking 'Fuck it, I am going anyway.' The next day I rang the airline and booked the next available flight to LAX. It was a real milk run of a flight—Perth to Kuala Lumpur to Japan to LAX— but I didn't care. It was the first available flight and I intended to be on it.

The Trip

I departed Perth Airport on the 31st of December 1999, and as it turned out, I got to see the turn of the millennium twice. Once on stopover in KL, then again mid-air between Japan and LAX when we crossed the international date line, taking us back to the 31st. It ticked over midnight and it was the New Year again. Malaysian Airlines handed out little paperweights with 'Millennium Flight' on it.

There wouldn't be too many people that can say they saw the turn of the millennium twice! Had I known I was going to be mid-air, with all the hype around the Y2K bug, I probably wouldn't have chosen that flight, but thankfully the Y2K hype was just that, and I figure they wouldn't have flown if it wasn't safe—right?

The jumbo landed in LAX, and for a young bloke from sleepy old Perth, the place was monstrous! I caught a cab to the nearest bus port, where I took a bus from LA to Kansas City. In retrospect, I should have flown. At the time, I thought it would be a good way to see the country, and it was much cheaper. BAD move—about 2700 km of bad. The buses were super cramped and uncomfortable. I was on and off, waiting for connecting buses, and in transit for days and nights.

Eventually, I arrived at the bus port in downtown Kansas City and caught a cab to a cheap motel in Lenexa, the suburb where Kristy lived.

Surprise

Up to this point, I had not told her that I was coming. I just figured I would surprise her.

When I arrived at the motel, I rented a room and fell into bed to catch up on some badly needed sleep. When I woke up I had a shower, got dressed and gave her a call at work. I played it cool as though I was calling from home in Perth as normal. We spoke for a while, catching up on the days I had missed. Then I dropped it on her. "Hey, guess what?" I said. "What?" she replied. "Did you notice how there's no delay on this phone line?" She went quiet, then finally said, "No". I followed up with, "Well, guess what..." She replied with another curious "what?". "I'm here," I told her. "Where?" she responded excitedly. "I'm in Lenexa!" I said. "No! Get out!" she said in disbelief. Eventually, I managed to convince her that I was just down the road. I gave her the address, she left work and jumped in her car.

About 15 minutes later I heard a knock on my door. My heart was pounding a million miles an hour, ready to explode. I let her in, both of us grinning stupidly like Cheshire cats. She was taller than I had imagined and she was gorgeous. We hugged instantly; I think I was too nervous to go in for the kiss, but the hug was blissful. Eventually, we separated and sat on the corners of opposing beds, mostly fumbling our way through nervous conversation for about half an hour.

I told her about the journey, she told me about her new job and what she had gone through. After what felt like an eternity, I felt comfortable enough to ask if I could kiss her. "I thought you'd never ask," she replied. It was on—gentlemen never tell, but it was the most amazing physical and spiritual connection I had ever experienced. I hadn't much experience up until then, but it was AMAZING! That first day we stayed in bed and loved, talked, laughed, slept, on repeat—until hunger got the better of us, so we went out for food.

Kristy still had to work by day to pay her father back, and he insisted she get home by 10pm. She didn't tell him about me for fear of upsetting him. By day she worked and I explored the area on foot, and we would catch up mornings, evenings and all weekend.

Even though we didn't go far from Kansas City, we had an amazing six weeks together; seeing the local sights, activities and dining out. I had only booked four weeks off work, and by six weeks, my boss was eager for me to come back. I was also starting to run out of money. After six weeks of cheap accommodation, all the eating out and activities, I had about $1000 left and still had to get back to LAX.

I wanted to stay so badly; she wanted me to stay too—I was torn. If I stayed I would have run out of money, had no job, no family, no friends to call on. We would have had to get married so I could stay as I had no work visa. To me, that was getting married for the wrong reason. Where were we going to live? What would I do for work? I would have been an illegal alien. It was the hardest decision I had ever made to date ... stay or go home.

Sliding doors moment 1 — Downhill

With too many unknowns if I stayed, I made the heartbreaking decision to return home to Perth. I left Kristy with $700, about half of what she needed for the airfare to Australia. I got on the bus back to LA in tears, and if I thought the bus trip from LA to Kansas was rough, the trip back to LA was ten times worse. I spent a lot of that journey in tears.

After what seemed like an eternity, I arrived back at LAX and had to stay at one of the nearby hotels to wait for my plane. I rang Dad from the hotel in tears, telling him I wanted to stay, secretly hoping he would tell me to stay and offer some money, but he told me to come home. So I did—I went home.

The next few months were bloody horrible. I was coming down from an amazing experience, and had to go back to work, officially out of money. I missed my girl so painfully. I didn't want to go out or see anyone. I was hugely depressed. The plan was that Kristy would work hard, pay her dad back, sell her car and then buy a ticket to Perth so we could be together again.

We still spoke and chatted online, but it just wasn't the same. Most conversations ended in tears which was depressing. The frequency of our calls and chats dropped off—we dropped off. We still loved each other dearly, but I think it was just too painful being apart. Months went by and I grew more depressed. My longing turned into frustration—why wasn't she coming? Looking back, there were probably a ton of reasons, but it felt fairly singular to me. Didn't she love me? As time passed, the communication all but stopped. I had resigned myself to the likelihood that she wasn't coming.

The suicide attempt

In my ever-diminishing circle of friends, 21st birthdays were a big deal. Usually the parents would throw a big party with lots of guests, food and drink, a touching speech and good times.

On the 28th of August 2000, it was my 21st birthday. My boss held a lunch for me with my work colleagues. My dad and his wife came too. I had a few too many drinks considering I still had to drive home after work. It was fun trying to work half-drunk though; I was a draftsman so operating a computer 'under the influence' was hardly dangerous, but somewhat of a challenge. Everyone at work was in good 'spirits'.

After work I didn't have any plans for my birthday night, so I grabbed a couple of six packs and headed home to my two-bedroom flat in Scarborough. I watched TV, drank my drinks, and feeling sorry for myself, broke down and sobbed uncontrollably.

Once the last can was gone, I got up off the couch, pulled my belt out of my work pants and looped the loose end through the buckle. I put the loop over my head and around my neck, walked up to the door, opened it, stood tall on tiptoes, and jammed the loose end of the belt over the hinge side corner of the door. I pulled the door shut and gave a couple of hard tugs to make sure it was stuck solid.

With tears in my eyes, I let my weight drop. The belt loop tightened hard around my neck—it hurt like hell, but I stuck with the pain. In the space of seconds, everything started to grey out and tingle.

Darkness ...

As I came to, everything was dark and tingling. I gasped for air, trying to scream for help, but nothing would come out. Seconds later, it hit me like a freight train—excruciating pain. My right leg must have buckled underneath me when I fell to the ground. I lay there in agony for what seemed like an eternity, crying, feeling so ashamed of what I had just done, and wondering what had just happened.

The shame and anger

I figured when I passed out that I may have convulsed, dropped or thrashed ... I don't know. I was unconscious, but the belt had slipped out of the door frame. Eventually, I commando crawled to the couch, pulled myself up and called my mum, who lived in Queensland at the time. I told her what happened. She was extremely concerned, and she offered to fly over immediately to be with me. But I reassured her that I was OK and had no plan to try again. I told her not to come; I felt so ashamed of myself. I didn't want a fuss or any help—I did this, I would clean it up.

The next day I went to the doctor and he sent me off for scans. I had completely torn a ligament in my right knee. The next major hurdle was to get that fixed, which meant surgery and a few weeks off work. Whenever anyone asked, I told them it was an old football injury that had flared up. I didn't tell the truth to anyone in my family for years, except for Mum. I didn't even tell Kristy what had happened. I was mad at Kristy for not coming, I was mad at Dad for not throwing me a 21st birthday party, I was mad at Mum for not coming to help—even though I told her not to. I was angry at myself for everything. I was just angry in general.

Tracey

In the time off work, which was late in September 2000, I returned to chatting online. What else was I going to do with my crippled time? This time I spoke with other people but only occasionally with Kristy. I had given up on her, even though she said she was still coming and still trying to save the money. I had opened the door to talking to other women, and that is when I met Tracey in a Perth locals chat room. We hit it off, had a good laugh, and soon met up. She had a son who was 18 months old at the time. I gave it a chance, when I probably shouldn't have, as I didn't want kids yet. We went out on a few dates, and things were fun and exciting, as they usually are when things are new and fresh.

After a couple of weeks dating Tracey, I had major problems with my computer. Tracey's parents had a computer business and she offered for her father to have a look at it.

The day Tracey returned my computer to me, she seemed a bit off, a bit strange. Later that night we got into an argument, and she admitted that when the computer was at her parent's place, she had looked at my private message history and emails with Kristy. I was mad at her for snooping through my private stuff, and she was mad at me for not telling her about Kristy. We had both done wrong, and that was a major break in trust on both sides.

Sliding doors moment 2 — Broken trust

In hindsight, I shouldn't have gone past that point with her. But we continued dating, and I secretly kept in contact with Kristy, mostly chat and email, without Tracey knowing. Around November that year, the flat in Scarborough that I was renting was sold and I was forced to find another place to rent. When I moved, Tracey and her son moved in with me. I remember feeling resistance within, but I reluctantly accepted it.

It was around this time that my beloved Pa passed away from an aneurysm—utter devastation. My grandfather, my mentor, my friend, was gone. I had seen him only a couple of weeks prior and he seemed happy and healthy at the time, so it came as quite a shock when he died.

Soon after moving into the new flat with Tracey and her son, I got an email from Kristy saying she had bought a plane ticket to Perth for a few weeks time. Oh fuck! What do I do now? I had moved in with the new girlfriend and my 'soulmate' was finally on her way. I was torn yet again. I decided to sleep on it.

Sliding doors moment 3 — Love the one you're with

Only a week or so before Kristy was due, I came clean with her. I told Kristy everything and said not to come. I can only imagine how it would have destroyed her; I know it killed a big part inside of me. I didn't tell Tracey all of this, but I had made my choice and life went on with her. We moved into a bigger house together. I went back to TAFE to study computer systems engineering and started working for Tracey's parents part-time, while still working full-time in my first drafting job.

In January 2002, Tracey and I bought our first house together. It was a bargain because the guy who owned it prior had killed his wife and buried her in the backyard. We purchased the house as a mortgagee sale and proceeded with superficial renovations; painting, surfaces, etc.

Soon after that, we got engaged.

On Valentine's day, February 14th, 2004, Tracey and I got married—romantic, right? Nothing to do with never forgetting an anniversary. It was a fun wedding with our friends and family. The day was perfect really—a perfectly expensive piss-up with a great honeymoon in Florida.

FIFO

After the honeymoon we returned to 'normal' life. I had a desire to earn more money and was lured into mining jobs up north as a Fly In Fly Out (FIFO) worker. People warned me that I was signing my own divorce papers by working away, but I wanted to give it a go, convinced the good money could set us up for life.

As it turned out the money was great; however, my relationship with my wife and stepson suffered BADLY.

I was on a terrible roster of five weeks on and one week off, and consequently, Tracey and my stepson got used to life without me. When I came home, I was more of a hindrance than a help. They had to adjust to life with me for one week then adjust again for the next five weeks away. It was brutal! And the work was HARD, working 12 to 14 hour days in 40-45°C heat.

Late 2004, Tracey and I had a big argument, and I left with a swag and a bottle of grog to go to a mate's place for his birthday party. I got trashed and slept in my swag on his back lawn. The next day when I got home, she tore strips off me for staying out all night without letting her know. I figured that as I had left with a swag and a bottle of booze, it was a logical outcome. For me, it was the straw that broke that camel's back—I called it quits, it was all over.

A new beginning with an old problem

I went and lived with a friend around the corner, while still working away. After a couple of months, Tracey had moved on with someone else. I wasn't upset that she had moved on, but I was upset that I hadn't had the time to move on myself. On my week off I was dealing with the grief of losing the relationship, and then onsite for five weeks, I was too busy and tired to deal with any of my problems, let alone try to move on. I was not coping, and depression had me once again, so I quit my FIFO job and relocated back to Perth.

Even though I enjoyed computers, the pay was relatively low, so I went back to drafting; this time designing semi-trailers. It was good money, on a better hourly rate than up north, just not as many hours, meaning much more time off. I started dating again with a few failed attempts and purchased a small house of my own.

Margret

In July 2005, I organised to have dinner with my cousin Bec to catch up. When I got to her flat, I found out that she had invited two of her high school friends to join us for dinner. One of them was already there and they were halfway through watching 'Big Brother'. Her name was Margret and she was gorgeous, so I sat on the adjoining couch and tried to play it cool. The show ended, and we went to a nice pub for dinner. I remember that Margret was so warm, friendly, bubbly and gorgeous—did I mention that? We all had a wonderful dinner together.

In the following days, I couldn't stop thinking about Margret; she was lovely, but I felt she was way out of my league. However, I figured I had nothing to lose, so why not have a crack? I texted

Bec for Margret's phone number and rang her, nervous as heck, and asked her out on a date. She said yes—you bloody ripper!

I took Margret on our first date. A word of advice for anyone going on a first date—do NOT eat chilli and do NOT wear sneakers! The chilli made me sweat profusely and my nose run badly, and sneakers, well, apparently that's just poor form.

It turned out Margret had just been through a break-up too, and neither of us was really looking for anything serious. Margret was a hippy at heart, a vegetarian environmentalist—not what I would have classed as my type at all—but she was hot. I, on the other hand, was a very conventional meat 'n' veg, capitalistic consumer.

We dated for six months and eventually, I asked Margret to move in with me.

The Pause

Unfortunately, something wasn't right with me—I was still depressed. I went to a psychologist to try sort that out and while a couple of months of therapy helped a little with the depression, it left me questioning so many aspects of my life. I didn't feel like I was happy or in control of my life while living with Margret, even though we were getting along. Consequently, I concluded that I needed to end the relationship. She moved out.

I cleaned up my act, started eating clean, read lots of self-help books and exercised. Margret and I had remained friends and we started doing Pilates classes together (Pilates—very manly indeed, but the view was good for a single man). After a couple of months on hiatus, we got back together.

I sold my house and moved in with a friend not far from where Margret was living, and eventually, she moved in with me again. Early in 2008 we got engaged, and by mid-2008 we started looking for a place of our own to buy. In November 2008, we married, and after our honeymoon, we moved into our new, old, one-bedroom flat.

In 2009, I was starting to feel unappreciated and taken for granted in my job. While life was pretty good, work was getting me down, and depression was rearing its ugly head yet again.

Charlie

In December 2009 Margret fell pregnant with our first child. One evening in September 2010, after a particularly rough day at work, I was feeling very upset. I walked in the door and said to Margret, "I hope this baby comes tonight because I do not want to go back to work tomorrow." Almost as if my unborn child had heard me, Margret went into labour, roughly two weeks early. It was a planned home birth with two midwives on hand. Our son, Charlie, was born in an inflatable birthing pool in the middle of the lounge room in our tiny 50 square metre flat. It was an amazing experience—I got to 'catch' my son when he was born. WILD!

Country life

After much searching, I got a job with an engineering company in the country. We embraced country life and loved it. In just a few months of living in the country, I knew more people there than years of living in the city. People know who you are in the country and look out for each other's kids. We did miss some of the conveniences and selection of shops and activities available in the city, but we made up for it in lifestyle and community and it was the perfect place for raising kids. Things ticked along nicely for a while, and although I wasn't getting paid what I felt I was worth, we still made a good living.

Mia

Two years later, in January 2013, our second child, Mia, was born in Perth, in the same inflatable birthing pool in my in-law's lounge room. This time I didn't get to 'catch' my daughter, but it was still a wonderful experience to hold my baby girl.

Mission - The old bowling club

In March 2013, we purchased the town's old lawn bowls clubhouse, which had been sitting derelict for several years. Structurally, the building was sound and we set about renovating it.

Meanwhile, I was feeling blue constantly. My eating grew out of control, and my weight ballooned, even though I was working physically hard on the renovations. I was having vivid nightmares of death, and the stress was immense. I went to the doctor who prescribed anti-depressants which helped a little, but they had some nasty side effects. They numbed the blues, but they also numbed my other senses.

The renovations took about 18 months and while it was tough working full-time and renovating part-time, we did it. The stress levels were incredibly high, and my attitude at work had started to slide as I felt undervalued and unappreciated—I wasn't enjoying life.

Downhill again

At the end of August 2014, we completed the renovations and moved in just before my birthday. Although it was fantastic moving into the 'new' place, I fell in a hole. I was exhausted; physically, mentally, emotionally, and stressed to the max. With the project complete, I lost my drive, and I felt guilty for missing so much time with my kids, especially Mia, since I had spent a fair bit of time with Charlie through his equivalent stage. I was struggling at work, dropping my hours back to cope, and I had more and more days off; both sick and just avoiding work—I didn't want to be there.

Over time, things got worse as my eating escalated further out of control. I wasn't exercising and my weight ballooned further. I struggled to get out of bed, even on weekends. I was massively depressed.

Logically, it made no sense. The stress of the renovation was gone. I had a great house, cars, an amazing wife and two beautiful kids. My job was relatively good; the money was good enough, and they were incredibly tolerant of my waning ways. I just wasn't happy there—I just wasn't happy anywhere. On paper it was all great, I had it all, but I was severely depressed. It made no sense.

The realisation

One day in October 2014, I remember struggling to get out of bed and go to work, but I did and the first thing I did when I sat down, was google 'suicide help'. I was having suicidal thoughts and struggling to hold back the tears. I picked myself up and went home, crawled back into bed and slept, knowing I needed help. I didn't want to commit suicide; I loved my wife and kids too much to do that to them. What sort of example would that set for my kids? Would I be teaching them that suicide is OK? It just wasn't an option. I had to get help—fast.

One of the results of that Google search at work was Palladium Private™. I had never heard of it before, but it sounded pretty good with on-site treatment in a retreat setting, and all sorts of alternative treatments and therapies. But despite my enthusiasm for this holistic option, I wanted a second opinion, so we went back to the doctor.

The first thing the doctor did was put me on the scales. At 141 kg I was the heaviest I had ever been. He then said, and I quote, "Let's address the elephant in the room shall we?" A great choice of words for a depressed person who just got off the scales. He then proceeded to lecture me that I was overweight and needed to consider gastric bypass surgery. My wife and I left shocked and in disbelief. We went in with severe depression and came out with a referral for surgery. That was not the help or advice that we needed or wanted.

We went home and researched Palladium Private™ and other options, like clinical psychology and psychiatry, and associated treatment facilities in Perth. Having no luck with various drugs up to that point, we both felt that more drugs would not help. We wanted to address the cause of the depression, not just mask the symptoms.

Help

Palladium Private™ was looking the best option as they advertised a VERY different philosophy. Their holistic approach included diet adjustments, exercise, relaxation, and treatments of both one on one and group sessions in a retreat environment. We rang them for more info, and they suggested a three-week stay. The treatment sounded great, and then they gave us the price—over $15,000, including flights to Queensland— OUCH! They were very confident of a positive outcome, but we didn't have that sort of money especially after the renovations. We did more research into other treatments and options, but our 'gut feeling' was to go with Palladium Private™.

In the end, we came clean with my dad about my depression and asked him for the money. At the beginning of November, I flew out to Queensland.

Treatment

It was tough, but I did the hard work that lay in front of me and in those three weeks in Queensland, I lost 16 kg, gained a new way of thinking, and a new set of tools for how to deal with things. Suffice to say, it worked VERY well.

Since attending Palladium Private™, I have lost a total of 27 kg at the time of writing. I have a new outlook on life, a new way of living, and a thirst for learning and personal growth. I am healthy and happy with who I am and where I am at in my life. I quit my job and started a design consultancy business. For a while there was still the occasional blue day, but the severity and longevity were much less thanks to the tools and techniques that I now have.

My truth

This book represents a manual of my learnings—it is my truth to date. It is what has worked for me, and worked well. While I hope to plant the seeds for your learning, don't take my word for any of it—try things for yourself, do more research and find your own truths. If YOU want change in your life, it is YOU who needs to make that happen, as ultimately, no-one can take responsibility for YOUR actions—they are YOURS alone.

A side note

In this introduction, I have tried to describe everything the way that I thought about them at that point in time. It was incredibly hard and emotionally draining to write the intro that way. After my journey, treatments and learnings, I am glad to say I do not think about anything the same way now. I am OK with my past and do not hold any ill-feelings against anyone mentioned in this book. My past is how I got to this point in my life, and I wouldn't change any of it. I hope you understand this by the end of the book.

Back to Basix

For many years, I searched for a solution to my problems, and until recently, I never found it. I was looking in all the wrong places. Looking for solutions outside of myself, I wanted others to fix me. "Tell me what's wrong, give me the magic pill, give me the quick fix, cut me open, anything, just fix me now and take my money. Please!"

Fail.

The problem with perceived solutions which come from outside of us, is that they are usually only 'band-aid' fixes that hide the symptoms without fixing the underlying problem. Sure, the band-aid hides the surface bleeding, but until we heal from within the bleeding won't stop. If you rip the band-aid off too soon, before you have healed, the blood just keeps coming. Similarly, you can take a pill for depression to feel better, but unless you heal the underlying issues, you cannot stop taking the pills without the depression coming back.

Sometimes we need help from others to show us the way, but when it comes to change and healing, the only person who can walk through that door is you. If you are not willing to change, all the assistance in the world cannot help you.

The solutions come from within, and they all spring from getting back to Basix. Yes, that spelling is correct. 'Basix' means basics, but it ends in six because there are six essential elements to build a better life.

No matter what your hopes, dreams and aspirations are in life, without the Basix, you can kiss them goodbye. Regardless of your current position in life, you need to work on improving and maintaining all of your Basix. Without a good foundation, you cannot build a solid house; similarly, without the Basix, you cannot build much of a life. If you get the Basix right, life takes off—almost like magic.

What are the Basix?
1. Choices, Decisions and Commitments
2. Goals, Habits and Growth
3. Thoughts and Beliefs
4. Food
5. Exercise
6. Peace of Mind

You may already be doing a cracking good job on some of these. Like many things in life, you can ignore one or two of these and get away with it, but eventually cracks will show in your foundations. When those foundations are subjected to extra stress, the fractures can turn into catastrophic failures, bringing down everything around you. It is imperative to build and maintain ALL six elements.

Before my treatment in 2014, I was regularly sick. If somebody sneezed in my general direction, I fell ill for days, if not weeks. Today my Basix are strong, and I have not had a full sick day since 2014. I have had the odd sniffle—recently I had a bout of gastro which had me bedridden for half a day. I still have the odd blue day, but with my ever-improving Basix and my new tools and techniques, these have been short-lived.

Taking care of the Basix does not mean that you will be infallible, or impervious to emotion or stress, but it reduces the severity and recovery from down-time, and gives you a greater sense of durability. Shit still happens in life; you just tend to bounce back quicker and easier.

Let's explore each of the Basix further.

Basix 1: Choice, Decision and Commitment

This may be one of the simplest concepts in this book, but it is by far the most important. Without this section, you may as well throw the book in the trash, because it is our choices, decisions and commitments that underpin ALL the other Basix. Without mastering this one element, you cannot truly follow through with the rest of the Basix.

Earlier I stated that 'the solutions come from within'. Well, I would like to expand that statement:

> **The solutions come from within; they start with a choice, are possible with a decision and happen with absolute commitment.**

Every choice comes down to this: Keep doing what I am doing and getting the same results, OR, change and face the unknown.

Pretty simple choice, right? Well, no.

It is the toughest funking choice in the world. We all struggle with it every day. Why is change so hard?

It is because our current state is what we *know*, it is our secure safety blanket that keeps us from facing what is hard, what is terrifying, the fear of the 'unknown' and the possibility of us being 'wrong'. Even though something may be bad for us, we keep on doing it because, on some level, it serves our needs.

Tony Robbins identifies six human needs:
- Certainty
- Variety
- Significance
- Connection
- Growth
- Contribution

Everything we do serves one, or more, of our needs. Each of us has one or two of these needs which we favour over the others. Even if there are adverse effects, where one need is gratified and another need is violated, the gratification of one priority need, outweighs the pain of compromising the other secondary needs. It is only when we can associate enough pain with an unwanted action or habit, that we can make changes.

For me, it was only when I could associate enough pain to being depressed or suicidal that I could create change. The increasing pain of feeling and looking like shit, leaving my family behind, missing my wife and kids, setting a terrible example for my kids, and so the list goes on. The pain of doing the same thing outweighed the fear of change—the DECISION was to change.

"Decisions, not conditions, determine your destiny."
Tony Robbins

A decision without a commitment is merely a hope!

Commitment is a funny thing. As the saying goes, '99% commitment is a bitch, 100% is a breeze'. If you are truly committed to a change, then there is no procrastination or chance of failure. The decision becomes easy, even if the path ahead is not. If you ever find yourself procrastinating, ask yourself 'how committed am I to doing this?'

Once I had made the decision to change, to get help and beat my depression, I was, and still am, 100% committed to that decision. It was possibly one of the hardest things I have ever been through; having to address my demons, my issues, eating, exercising, beliefs, habits and peace of mind. I will never go back to the 'old' way of living because I know where it leads, and I will be fucked if I will let that happen again.

Every day we must be vigilant with the choices we face, especially when related to the other Basix. We must make decisions and commitments to move us in the direction we desire.

Figure out what it is you truly want, then make the decision with a 100% commitment to change. If you have trouble following through, look at how you are serving your needs by NOT following through, and find ways to associate massive pain to NOT making the commitment to change.

For example, if you want to lose weight, yet you have trouble following through with doing so, look at what needs are being met while you are sabotaging your efforts. Is it the certainty of an excessive food supply? Is it the certainty of comfort that the food provides? Or the certainty of staying the same? Is it the fear of what people might think of you trying?

Look at all aspects, and when you find reasons for why you may be sabotaging yourself, you need to figure a way to associate massive pain to not losing weight. Come up with creative ways of doing so, and look at all the consequences of NOT losing weight.

Play the game of living in the future, looking back on now and see what you wish you had done today, and why. Find the biggest, nastiest reason to lose weight and amplify it with some creative imagination.

Imagine weighing 250 kg, sick and unable to move, stuck in a hospital bed, waiting to die. What thoughts do you think might run through your head when a nurse is cleaning up your shit because you can't make it to the toilet? 'If only I had lost weight, if only I had taken control of my life.'

Whatever scares the shit out of you, visualise that in your head every morning when you wake up and every night before you go to bed.

The above is only an example, but you get the idea. You must find and amplify the pain associated with not following through, then commit 100% to making the change you desire.

Life is choice, bro.

Quality of Decisions

Whenever we are faced with a tough choice, it is possible to get bogged down in the process and ultimately avoid making the decision altogether.

> *"Successful people make decisions quickly (as soon as all the facts are available) and change them very slowly (if ever). Unsuccessful people make decisions very slowly, and change them often and quickly."*
>
> *Napoleon Hill*

When making a tough decision, it is important to consider the following:

1. Do I have all the information I need to make a good decision or are there major holes in the data? If possible, get the missing information before deciding.

2. What are the foreseeable outcomes and how do they fit with my higher goals, principles and values? Usually, we need to choose what fits best with those goals.

3. Are the costs (time, money, effort, etc.) worth the possible benefits (achievement, profit, happiness, etc.)?

4. Are the worst-case scenarios as bad as they seem? What measures can be put in place to minimise the severity? More often than not, if you can set aside your fears, the worst cases are never as bad as they seem.

5. How will 'future me' feel about having made the decision for this outcome?

6. Is the decision or action reversible, and is there a backup plan in case things don't go to plan?

The biggest question when making any decision is to ask 'is the outcome of this decision going to align with my higher goals, principles and values?'

In any decision, you need to hope for the best, consider the worst, decide, then give it your everything—100% commitment. You will make mistakes along the way, but that is part of the 'try, learn, grow, repeat' process.

Your head is a computer, your heart is a guide

You can be the most analytical person in the world and break the decision-making process right down to ensure you are making the correct logical choice, but ultimately you have to live with the consequences of that decision.

Sometimes, when we make a logical decision based on all of the information and parameters available, the decision may feel off. The head has said yes, but the heart or gut is saying no (or vice versa). The head's decision may still be the correct one, but if the heart or gut feeling is not right then it is definitely worth a review of the decision, this time looking at the emotional and social costs of that decision. Is anyone likely to be hurt by the result of the decision? What consequence will this decision have on my relationships? Will my integrity remain intact? Will I be violating any of my core values?

Money comes and goes, but relationships are harder to repair.

Improve the quality of your questions

Any question that you feed that biological supercomputer (brain), it will automatically set about finding and generating answers.

If you ask it a shitty question, such as 'What's wrong with me?', it will give you a set of shitty answers to match, like 'You are dumb, you just can't handle pressure, you are full of excuses, your word doesn't count for shit', and on and on it will go until you give it another question.

If you ask it shit-hot questions, such as 'How can I make this happen?', it will set about getting you a set of shit-hot answers, like 'Formulate a plan, make more money, get help' and on it goes.

Five great shit-hot questions to constantly ask:
1. What is the better question I could be asking? There is always a better question, which will lead to better answers.
2. On my deathbed, what option would make me most proud?
3. What advice would I give to my child if they were in the same situation? Even if you don't have a child, try to imagine that you did, and what would you see as the best result for them? It may bring out inner wisdom.
4. What is it that I REALLY want? Not what you think you want, but what is the underlying desire? 'I want to be rich', could have an underlying desire of financial freedom to do what you want (there is a big difference—rich doesn't mean free if you have to keep feeding mortgages).

5. What are my other options? Often, we get bogged down in choosing one or two things, oblivious to the possibility of other possible options.

"Questions provide the key to unlocking our unlimited potential. Quality questions create a quality life. Successful people ask better questions, and as a result, they get better answers."

Tony Robbins

Fear

Often, a decision can be an obvious one, yet we shy away from it because of fear; the fear of consequences, the fear of what others may think, do or say; the fear of failure, the fear of loss. Our safety mechanisms and over-compensations kick in to keep us from making 'bad' decisions. If you look at the worst case scenarios of any decision, more often than not, they aren't that bad and are usually reversible.

Use fear as a guiding light to move towards, rather than a lighthouse to avoid. Lean into fear and do what it is that has you fearful or anxious. This one change has made an amazing difference in my life.

What's in the way, is the way

In the past, I was a classic 'deferrer'. Whenever something bothered me, I would avoid or ignore the problem and over time I would sit on it, hoping it would just go away. Instead, it would fester inside, growing in intensity, at least until it happened again, and then I would erupt with an over-the-top explosion of emotion. And everyone around is left thinking WTF?!

My life coach taught me a saying which I have found incredibly powerful: *'What's in the way, is the way'*

What this means is that if you have a problem, issue, decision, emotion, thought or bodily sensation that is constantly bothering you, it needs to take priority and you need deal with it. If you don't deal with it there and then, it will start to adversely affect other aspects of your life.

The exception to this rule is if you are overly angry or emotional in the heat of the moment. Take five, cool down, and then, with a level head, return to deal with the problem.

If something or someone is bothering you, it is best to deal with it immediately, before it gets out of control, or you turn into a volcano ready to erupt.

Integrity

Without it, you don't have shit—integrity is everything. If you get caught lying, cheating, stealing or scamming just once, you are done, if not imprisoned. Word gets around like lightning that you have done wrong; you just flushed your reputation and trust down the shitter. Even if you don't get caught, you will forever be wondering when, not if, you will get busted. Not only that, you can't hide that you are a 'rat', as what is on the inside tends to show on the outside through micro-expressions, behaviour and body language. It is just downright easier to live with honesty and integrity.

If you have lived your past without integrity, now is a great time to start—it IS that easy. You may have already lost your reputation, but if you own your mistakes and keep living with honesty and integrity, eventually people will come around. Remember, what is on the inside, will show.

What is the next step? And just keep chewing

Once you have made any decision and backed it with 100% commitment, then it is time to start DOING. You don't need to have a definite plan. In fact, a full and detailed plan can get you bogged down and you may suffer paralysis by analysis and never achieve anything.

A better way to go is to always ask this golden question: 'What is the next step?'

Once you have answered that, DO that step, then ask it again and DO it again. Repeat until you succeed.

Here's a great lesson that my father taught me, and that his father taught him, to overcome the overwhelm of getting something done.

> *"If you have a plate full of food (that you absolutely must get through), just keep chewing. Otherwise you will choke."*

So, once you have made a decision, just keep asking, 'What is the next step?' and then just keep chewing.

Basix 2: Goals, Habits and Growth

"Either you're growing or you're decaying; there's no middle ground. If you're standing still, you're decaying."   Alan Arkin

Remember that saying. Life is learning, growing and reaching, then repeating.

Once you have decided and committed to a decision for change, achievement or attainment, it is then time to set in place the goals, habits and plans for that growth.

Goals

Back in 1999, I set a goal of planning and paying for a trip to the USA to meet my internet girlfriend (see the introduction). I set a specific, measurable, achievable, realistic, time-based (SMART) goal—although I didn't know that's what it was at the time—and I smashed it hard.

I set a plan in place, and there was no chance for failure because I wanted it so badly. I was 100% committed. Despite a major hiccup before departure, I still fulfilled my goal. It was an awesome feeling to know that I could achieve whatever I wanted in life. The goal was a success, and I have always been proud of it. The goal itself was a positive experience.

However …

In 2013, I set myself another massive goal of renovating a derelict old building into a home for my family. Another (SMART) goal that I smashed hard and achieved. This time after completion I didn't get that same sense of fulfilment—I fell into a mental hole and couldn't get out. I was in a funk. How was this possible? Financially it was a much bigger goal, time-wise it took two years and a shitload of hard work. The house is amazing. I should have felt even better about this goal, it was a much bigger achievement, but no ... WTF?!

What is the difference between the two major goals?

It was all about my self-worth, and where I had placed it.

In 1999 I didn't give a shit what anyone else thought of my goal. It was purely for me. I wasn't attaching my self-worth to anyone else's opinion, comments, or reactions—I was worthy regardless.

In August 2014, when I finished the house and we moved in (goal complete), I wasn't given the appreciation, admiration or accolades from others that I was hoping for. Nobody seemed to care—and in acceptance, nor should they. I had placed my self-worth purely in the hands of others and when I didn't get the recognition I was hoping for, I felt like I wasn't good enough. I felt worthless and I rode that pony all the way to Depression Town. Granted, the long exposure to physical and mental stress was a major factor, but I dealt with that OK for two years. It was this setback in self-esteem which sent me 'down the rabbit hole'.

Goals are a double-edged sword. There are so many benefits to goals, and I think that they are very important for motivating us in the right direction, but we need to be super vigilant about where we place our self-worth in relation to those goals. Do not attach your self-worth to the reactions of others. Remember that you are worthy regardless of whether you achieve a goal or not.

This is especially true if you don't hit your goals, and believe me, that happens to all of us. If we deviate from the path to achievement, we start to worry and stress about getting back on track. 'Shit is not going to plan' and this causes stress.

We need to upgrade shitty beliefs about failed goals to 'Life is a journey, full of ups and downs and I am worthy regardless.' This shit-hot upgrade helps to reduce stress around not achieving our goals. For more on this see Basix 3: Thoughts and Beliefs.

Even if you don't hit your goal, often you are still miles ahead of where you were before you started. Even if the result is a complete failure, you have learned a LOT of lessons along the way. This is valuable life learning, applicable to moving forward with your life. You are still worthy.

Use goals as a guide, never attach your self-worth to them.

Failure

Whatever we do in life, failure is a big part of it, so accept it and embrace it. It is how we learn; it is how we grow to rise and overcome, or avoid obstacles in the future.

We didn't learn to run overnight. As a baby we first learnt to walk by trying to get up off the ground and repeatedly falling, eventually figuring out how to balance and develop muscle control. Once we learnt to balance, then we had to repeat the process for taking steps, letting go, walking, jogging and then running. It was a long-ass process! How many times did we fall or fail in that process? Shitloads.

Accept in life that we fail more than we succeed. Fail fast, fail often and never attach your self-worth to any failure. Fail, learn, grow and advance.

Habits

Goals are very important to give us direction and motivation. With any significant goal, it may take time, money and effort to make it happen. Often, life just gets in the way, slowing us down, or stopping us all together. We need to work hard at our goals on a regular basis to make them happen.

Habits are an effective way to turn our goals into a reality. Without habits, we just amble our way through life sometimes remembering, sometimes forgetting, sometimes procrastinating, sometimes getting distracted from what is important to us.

Once you have a goal and commit to it 100% (remember 99% is a bitch, 100% is a breeze), set about identifying and forming regular habits that will put you on 'autopilot' to achieving those goals. Let's look at some examples:

Goal:	Habits to form to make it happen:
Weigh ?? kg	• Eat clean every day • Drink two big glasses of water first thing every morning and 6-8 glasses more every day • Exercise every day • Weigh yourself every day at the same time to track your progress • Keep daily meals to an 8-hour window
Save a deposit for house	• Invest $200 every week into compounding investments/funds/accounts • Work a second job three nights a week (for extra income to save) • Record every dollar spent every day to see where you can save money
Write a book	• Allocate 1 hour every day to writing at least one page

Develop mental toughness	• Take a 5-minute cold shower first thing every morning • Meditate 10-20 minutes every day • Journal your limiting beliefs for ½ hour every night
Renovate a house	• Work on the house 1-2 hours, five days a week

Habits can be difficult to get into at first, as we often have to adjust or break old habits and routines to fit in the new habits. It takes two to three weeks of consistent daily repetition of a habit for it to become automatic and ingrained into your routine. Once a habit is cemented, it takes very little will-power to maintain the habit—you will be on 'autopilot' to success.

If you set the right habits in place, you can almost forget the goals. If you do the habit consistently, you can't help but hit your goals. Your success becomes a positive side effect of your regular habits.

Use systems to help you with your habits. Use habit tracking apps to get you going (I used an app called 'Habit List'), use automated payments to isolated bank accounts to save money—for whatever you want to do, there are systems available to help. You need to make it easy and convenient for yourself to initiate and stick with the habit.

You don't get something for nothing! If you are 100% committed to a goal, you must form the regular habits of DOING the things required to achieve your goals.

Roll all of your required habits into a daily/weekly schedule and stick to it, without too much deviation, consistently for two to three weeks.

Here is my daily routine:

Time	Habit	Reason
5.00am	Wake up	Good time for me to do my habits and still get to work on time.
5:01am	Move my body: push-ups and sit-ups or 'Body by Science' and a walk	Goal: weigh 100 kg. Feel good, get the blood pumping, wake up, gain muscle definition.
6:15am	Cold shower 5 minutes	Goal: Complete 30 day cold shower challenge to build mental toughness.
6:30am	Drink 2 large glasses of water and take supplements (no breakfast)	Hydrate for the day ahead. Intake trace minerals. Goal: weigh 100 kg via 'the 8-hour diet.'
6:45am	Meditate 10-20 minutes	Build mental toughness and peace of mind.

Time	Habit	Reason
7:00am	10 ideas	Goal: Become an Idea Machine – James Altucher Choose Yourself Idea Challenge.
7:15am	Visualisation and Gratitude	Build positivity by focusing on the good things in life. Past, present and future.
7:30am	Creative work	Develop creative faculties.
8:00am	Start work	Make money to pay the bills.
12:00pm	Lunch	First meal of the day— typically cold meat and salad.
6:00pm	Family dinner	Build family bond by us all eating together.
6:30pm	Bath the kids ready for bed	Fatherly duties.
6:45pm	Read to kids	Positive experience of reading for the kids.
7:00pm	Kids into bed	So the kids get a good night's sleep.
Check	Eat clean for the day?	Goal: weigh 100 kg.
Check	Facilitate relationships?	Call someone to build better relationships.

Time	Habit	Reason
7:30pm	Personal Development – learn something new	Self-improvement to build a better life. Creativelive.com, Lynda. com, book summaries, etc.
8:30pm	Start getting ready for bed	Time to prepare for bed routine
9:00pm	Into Bed – reading	Time to wind down and relax before going to sleep. Time with the wife.
10.00pm	Lights out	To get 8 hours of sleep every night aiding peace of mind.

Do you feel like you don't have time to form any habits? Beware the bad habits. Do you watch a lot of TV or movies? Surf the internet a lot? On Facebook, Twitter, Snapchat or other social networks a lot? Then you are wasting a LOT of time in your day, time you could better use to develop your goals or your mind, rather than numb it.

If you miss a day of your habit, don't be hard on yourself. Smile, acknowledge, return to them and re-commit.

The 1% rule

All of my life I have 'tried' to improve myself and until a couple of years ago, I didn't do a very good job of it. I read a heap of self-help books, listened to audiobooks, went to seminars, etc. I wanted to improve my life. I had the knowledge, so why was I still failing? I was still getting fatter, I felt worse about myself, and in general, I was going backwards.

In today's world of instant gratification, everyone wants everything, now! I was no different. I wanted to make a change, many changes, and I wanted that change to be instant. I would set about trying to instil a change and go hard at it, almost obsessively. But almost always the pain of making the change became too much, so I would quickly give up and beat the shit out of myself for failing or quitting … again …

The best way I have found to make a change is to simply slow down, try to improve yourself or your outputs by just 1%, which is a very small percentage. You could almost argue that it is insignificant and if so, then what's the point? Well, if you can aim to improve just 1% a day it makes the task easier. Forget the end goal, find the habit that you need to achieve your goal, apply the habit, then try to increase your output by just 1% every day. The change is so small that it's easy to do, but over time the compounding effect of that 1% increase makes a massive difference at the end of a year.

Some days you will cream it and improve 10-20% instantly, other days you will go backwards, badly. When you do go backwards, just do the best you can anyway, then carry on the next day. You will have up days and down days—that is life. Remember, it is the average over time that is important and 1% improvement is the aim.

Here's a simple example of the 1% rule in use. Do you want to be able to do fifty push-ups straight, but ten is too hard?

Then every morning when you jump out of bed, whip out five short stroke push-ups—simple. Set yourself a target that is so easy that it's barely even a chore. If it is easy to do, then it is easy to start and build the habit. Each day increase the number of push-ups by 1%. Mathematically, in 233 days (7.8 months) you will be up to 50 push-ups straight. But I am willing to bet that you will hit 50 much sooner than that.

Push-ups are just an example, this principle can be applied to any area of change or improvement you want, whether it be exercise, money, weight, food, communication, swimming, etc. To set a habit, aim for a very low output level, then aim for a 1% improvement every time, and the hard thing becomes easier.

Recommended habits to develop

Exercise your 'Idea Muscle'

Two very good books to exercise the brain are James Altucher's *Choose Yourself!* and his wife Claudia Azula Altucher's book *Become an Idea Machine*. James introduces the idea of exercising your 'idea muscle', and Claudia takes it a step further and writes a whole book about it, with a shitload more information and suggestions on the subject. They are bloody brilliant books.

James and Claudia's claim is that one of the most important

things you can do for yourself is to become an idea machine. To do this, and just like any muscle we wish to build, we must exercise our 'idea muscle' daily.

Their suggestion is to come up with 10 ideas every day, relating to a particular subject, or even a random subject. Then take it a step further with 'idea sex', where you cross-pollinate two separate ideas to make a new one. The 10 ideas don't necessarily have to be good ones; the plan is just to practice coming up with ideas to 'exercise the idea muscle'. After a few months of 10 ideas, you will notice the quality of ideas increase. When you do come up with an idea you particularly like or resonates with you, then ACT on that idea and DO something to action it.

Develop an attitude of gratitude and appreciation

Incorporate a daily gratitude practice into your life—it could be as little as five minutes in bed when you wake up. Kicking your brain off by looking for the positives and expressing gratitude can set your day up wonderfully. I know that when I woke up in the depth of my depression, I was diving straight into the negatives. I wish I had known then what I know now and could apply this back then. In time, with the practice of gratitude, you will find yourself doing this by default and just 'being' grateful in the moment.

I do my daily gratitude practice straight after my meditation, and again with my family at dinner time, when we all take turns to be grateful for something—the kids love it. I can tell you that it has made a MASSIVE difference to my life and outlook!

Develop mental toughness

Mental toughness can be built, just like any other muscle in your body. It takes regular exercise to work your mind and make it stronger and more resilient to adversity. As you will learn in Basix 6: Peace of Mind, meditation is to the mind what exercise is to the muscles.

Another way which may sound a bit cuckoo, but extremely powerful for building mental toughness, is when you have your daily shower, forego the hot water. Yep, stone cold, for a good 5 minutes. The initial 30 seconds to 2 minutes is basically sheer terror! At first, it's hard not to squeal like a little girl, and that's if you can breathe at all! After a couple of minutes, it becomes somewhat bearable, and after 4 minutes, you're kind of numb and shivering. After you get out of the shower, you feel bloody cold, but typically within a couple of minutes you begin to feel more normal.

Challenge yourself to do this for 30 days straight. The reason is to build mental toughness. The premise is that if you can't handle 5 minutes of the discomfort of cold water, how can you possibly handle the discomfort of personal confrontations, meetings, tough decisions, etc?

As well as building mental toughness, the other benefits of cold shower therapy are diverse:
- It wakes you up, very quickly!
- Good for hair and skin.
- Improves immunity and circulation.

- Aids weight loss.
- Aids muscle soreness and recovery.
- Reduces inflammation.
- Eases stress.
- Helps relieve depression.

I did the 30 day cold shower challenge in the middle of winter in rural Western Australia where temperatures occasionally fell below freezing. Needless to say, the water was bloody cold! But you do get used to it—somewhat. After the 30 days, I have backed off to just a couple of minutes, just long enough to get clean, but still on full cold. It is now summer and compared to winter, a cold shower is a walk in the park, but it still feels great—afterwards.

Visualisation

Another very powerful practice is to visualise what it is you desire and to feel grateful that you already have it, even before you do. This works with the 'law of attraction', when your mind becomes ingrained with the visions of what you desire—it goes about looking for and creating opportunities and ways and means to make it happen. It may sound like 'rah-rah' crap, but think about it logically and without any stigma. How can your brain possibly get you what you want if you don't have a clear idea of what it is you want, or what it looks or feels like?

Another helpful tool here is to make a vision board. If you see an image of something you like, then photograph, clip, copy, and stick, pin or tape it onto a corkboard so you can look at it daily and again feel gratitude that you already have it—it is on its way.

Try a daily visualisation practice. Again, just 5 minutes before bed, so your brain can work on it while you sleep.

Creativity

Take up a creative hobby, even if you don't consider yourself creative. My belief is that we are all creative—some of us know how to do it, most of us don't. Doing something creative, in a similar way to the '10 ideas' exercise, develops different areas of the brain. Find something that you enjoy doing, something that appeals to you, or try different things.

Examples: Write a book, write a blog, draw a picture, colouring in, painting, airbrushing, metal or wood crafts, pottery, photography, fabric crafts, something, anything, that gets the creative juices going.

Don't be concerned with being a perfectionist—the practice here is just to practise. The skill isn't so important; it's the regular creative outlet which is. When you create something, you bring something new to the world, something different, something of you. If you stick with it long enough, you may even want to show it to the world.

Lifelong learning

For a while I had forgotten the joy of learning new things. I would do my 8-10 hours of work each day, come home, plonk my ever expanding arse on the couch and numb my mind away, watching a handful of TV series or movies. I had no interest in learning new things; I thought that I enjoyed watching TV, but no matter what I watched, when I turned it off I had this hollow feeling like I had just been spun a story which had zero bearing on my life. I also felt guilty for literally flushing my time down the drain, especially when I had just watched something craptacular. I wanted my two hours back.

These days I am on a complete media ban. With the time I have saved, I now use it to 'sharpen the tools' by learning new things. I might read a book or two, take an online class, watch a documentary, listen to an audiobook or work on my 'side hustle'. Anything to advance my goals and vision.

When you learn new skills and information, combined with the '10 ideas' habit, your brain automatically starts coming up with some pretty funky ideas. You can cross-pollinate areas of interest and see where the ideas take you.

If you are of the opinion that nothing interests you or there is nothing you want to learn, then I would strongly suggest looking at what floated your boat as a kid, as a teenager, or any hobbies you have had in the past.

The world is a wonderful place with so many new technologies and learning opportunities. Explore the wonder, as learning is growth. If you're not growing, you're stagnating or decaying. Your mind is a biological learning machine, so feed it with fun and interesting stuff. You can learn anything you want—get into it.

Get some sun

Forget tanning beds—it is just not natural! Get some healthy sun exposure without getting burnt, simply because sunburn hurts.

> *"We are designed, cell by cell, as creatures of the sun. Virtually every organ system in your body is dependent on sunshine for optimal performance."*
>
> Al Sears

As part of your daily practice, make some time to get 15-30 minutes of sun exposure in the morning or afternoon.

Basix 3: Thoughts and Beliefs

In 2014 at the peak of my depression, my head was all over the place. I had trouble stringing congruent thoughts together, I didn't feel appreciated at work, and my self-esteem was at rock bottom. I was concentrating on all the bad things in my life, and this created a self-perpetuating loop of self-loathing, stress and depression. I wanted to give up because I felt worthless.

We need to be aware of our thoughts, particularly those that cause us to feel stress or unwanted emotions. If we feel an unwanted emotion, we need to ask ourselves the golden question 'What must I be thinking to feel this way?'. All stressful or emotional thoughts come from four shitty beliefs that cause us stress. Underpinning all of these beliefs is a wish that something was different, but we will get to that.

A great resource on this topic is the book *28 Days to Beat the Blues: A Practical Guide To Reducing Stress* by Michelle Mark and Wayne Parrott. It's based on the Fountainhead Method™ that they taught us at Palladium Private™.

An interesting thought about stress: there is no such 'thing' as stress, but everyone feels it when there is a perceived threat. Think about that. Your brain processes events via your beliefs, resulting in bodily and emotional responses. It is only because of your responses that you 'feel' stress. You create the stress within your mind because of your beliefs. Someone or something else didn't give it to you; it's how you reacted. Alter your beliefs and that in turn alters your stress.

What do you think a toddler would do if it saw a lion in the wild? Probably want to go and pet the big kitty. What about as an adult? Run or hide. Who feels stress at seeing the lion? The toddler or the adult? The only difference here is the belief about what lions do, a belief which is formed through learning and experience.

Putting this into a computer science analogy—your brain is a biological supercomputer, it is the hardware. Your beliefs are the software, programmed from lifelong learning via external inputs and experiences. Your thoughts, decisions and actions are all outputs from those programmed beliefs.

Everything you do is driven by your beliefs. Most beliefs are established in early childhood, formed by experiencing your immediate environment and family member's actions and reactions to events. Experiences and learning create, re-enforce or contradict your beliefs.

Two people who experience the same event may react very differently depending on their beliefs. In any situation, you may have several conflicting beliefs about an event. It is your priority belief that always wins out.

Every unwanted emotion is caused by a thought, and that thought is formed by a programmed set of four shitty beliefs that cause us stress.

The Wishing Way: The four shitty beliefs that cause stress

I call these four shitty beliefs the 'Wishing Way' because all of them come back to a WISH that something was different. The gap between what we desire and what is real is what causes us stress—we are focusing on the gap that cannot be closed. Remember this:

Wishing that something was different causes us stress.

1. **'Shit is not going to plan.'** This shitty belief is that things aren't going to plan, even if we do everything possible to correct course. Even though you cannot possibly get back on track, you WISH you could, and this thought causes stress. Example: "I have lost my job, and the bank is foreclosing on me. I wish I could find another job to pay my mortgage and bills."

2. **'Missing out on shit.'** This shitty belief is that by choice or circumstance you are now missing out on something that you WISH you could have. You WISH you could change the choice or circumstance so that you don't miss out, which causes you stress. Example: "My grandfather died, I miss him so much, I wish I could have him back."

3. **'Should have done shit differently.'** This shitty belief is that you or somebody else should have done something differently in the past. You WISH you could change what was done in the past and this thought causes you stress. Example: "Dad shouldn't have sent me to that school, it was horrible."

4. **'I am a piece of shit.'** This shitty belief is that you feel your value as a person is degraded. You WISH you could change yourself and this thought causes you stress. Example: "I am so stupid, what an idiot."

What can we do about these four shitty beliefs that cause us stress? We apply some 'shit-hot' upgrades to those shitty beliefs. Just to clarify, 'shit-hot' is Aussie slang for 'great'—not a fresh hot pile of poo.

The Acceptance Way: Four shit-hot belief upgrades

I call this set of four upgrades the 'Acceptance Way' because all the upgrades ACCEPT the reality of 'what is'. EVERYONE makes mistakes; good or bad, there is value and opportunities that arise out of every situation, we just need to keep looking for the upside. Remember:

Accepting 'what is' helps to reduce our stress.

1. **'Shit does happen.'** Life is a rollercoaster full of ups and downs. This acceptance upgrade surrenders the wish to change what has happened, instead accepting 'what is' and making the most of the situation. The past is gone—simple. Use the experience to learn and look for the upside or opportunities. This acceptance and letting go of the past helps to reduce stress. Example: We apply an upgrade to shitty belief 1 as listed above. "My life is a journey, and even though I have lost my job and house, I am still here! I still have my health. I now have a blank canvas to start again!"

2. **'I gain when I lose shit.'** There is value in every experience. This acceptance upgrade acknowledges what happened when we 'missed out', accepting that it can't be changed. No matter how bad the experience was, there is usually some learning or opportunity attached to this experience. Concentrating on the upside or opportunities helps to reduce stress. Example: We apply an upgrade to shitty belief 2 as listed above. "Even though my grandfather is gone, I am very grateful for having had him in my life. He has taught me a lot, and I have many great memories to cherish. Everyone dies, it is a part of life's journey. I will make the most of the time I have left with other loved ones."

3. **'We did the best we could with the shit we had.'** We always do the best we can, with what we have at the time. This acceptance upgrade realises that you simply cannot go back in time to change things. You, or they, would still make the same choice, because at that time, with the information, beliefs and priorities you had, you did what you thought was 'right'. Accepting that everyone does the best they can at the time helps to reduce stress. Example: We apply an upgrade to shitty belief 3 as listed above. "My Dad did the best he could sending me to that school, he didn't know what it was like. He did what he thought was best for me. It could have been worse—I could have no education at all. There were also a lot of good memories to hang on to."

4. **'I am always shit-hot'** I am always worthy. This acceptance

upgrade is that no matter your position in life, you have the same inherent value as any other human being. You are alive, and that is a true gift and a miracle. Accepting the belief that you are always worthy helps to reduce stress. Example: We apply an upgrade to shitty belief 4 as listed above. "I made a mistake that I can learn from. Everyone makes mistakes, it's a part of learning. I am always worthy."

Now how do we apply those upgrades?

Journalling to upgrade your beliefs

The process of upgrading your beliefs can be challenging at first, and takes quite a bit of practice, but rest assured, the process does get easier with experience.

Think of an event that causes you a lot of stress or emotion, then write it down with all the colourful language, emotions, anger, hatred, whatever you feel. Let yourself feel ALL of the emotion intensely in the process. Getting the story out and expressing yourself fully can help immensely. Nobody has to read it—so 'let it rip, tater chip'. It can even be beneficial to burn it all when you've finished the upgrading process, as a symbolic gesture of release.

Once it is all down on paper, we analyse, identify and circle our wording and phrases that associate with the four shitty beliefs that cause us stress.

Then with a fresh sheet of paper, re-write the event, applying the appropriate upgrades to the circled shitty beliefs. A positive or optimistic upgrade must be applied, not just replaced with another shitty belief.

When you read your upgraded event, check if it still raises any emotion or physical response. If it does, this is a good indication that you may have to go through this process again with different real upgrades to the shitty beliefs.

That was only a quick summary of the process, so let's look at it in more detail:

Upgrade Step 1 – Write it out in full

Choose an event, memory or situation that causes you stress or emotion, one that you would like to feel differently about. Find a quiet place and some time to yourself, where you are unlikely to be interrupted. With a pen and some writing paper or journal, write the event, memory or situation out in full. Include all of the colourful descriptives, thoughts and feelings associated with it. While writing it all down, let yourself experience all of the emotions fully. Just get it all out on paper, the more thorough, the better.

Upgrade Step 2 – Read and body scan

When you feel like you have finished writing it all down, read it to yourself, feeling all of the emotions associated and check what bodily responses arise for you. Do you feel a tension in your gut? Do you feel a knot in your throat? Do you tear up or break down completely? Do you grit your teeth? Check for anything physical that arises from thinking about the stressful event or thought. This awareness of your bodily response is great for monitoring in the future, especially to assess if your thoughts and beliefs are causing you stress. You may need to upgrade on the spot, but we will get to that later.

Upgrade Step 3 – Analyse

Once you have checked your bodily responses, study what you have written. Look for words or phrases that are associated with the four shitty beliefs described earlier. Circle all of those words, phrases or sentences, then write the number of the applicable shitty belief next to each circle with a 1, 2, 3 or 4.

Some examples of language to look out for aligning with each of the shitty beliefs:

1. Not going to plan: 'I messed up, it didn't work out, I failed.'
2. Missing out: 'I miss, I was left behind, I lost.'
3. Should have/could have: 'I should have, he could have, I wish she would have.'
4. Worth-less: 'I am a loser, what an idiot, I feel like a moron.'

Upgrade Step 4 – Assess

You may notice a pattern arise out of your analysis. I remember when I went through this the first time, I had a huge number of 3's (should have/could have), blaming and wishing I/they could do things differently. My second highest were the number 2's (missing out). This may give you some insight as to which shitty beliefs may be dominant in your belief system, and what upgrades you need to focus on.

Upgrade step 5 – Re-write with upgrades

On a fresh sheet of paper, re-write the story, expressing the acceptance, positives or opportunities in each of the previous circles and apply the upgrades. Be careful not to use alternative shitty beliefs to replace the previous shitty beliefs, they must be positively worded acceptance based upgrades.

Upgrade Step 6 – Read the re-write and body scan

Read your new story and see if there is any residual negative emotions, feelings or bodily reactions that keep popping up. If there is, this is a good indication that you have not fully accepted 'what is' and you may need to go through this process several times until the emotions and bodily responses dissipate.

Upgrade Step 7 – Repeat if necessary

It may take several attempts to change your feelings about that event, memory or situation. Give yourself a decent break between attempts to let your subconscious process the 'new' reality. In the subsequent attempts, try and write it differently each time. You may find other truths or issues that arise.

Upgrade like a Jedi Knight

This process is not easy, but with time and practice you will become quite efficient at this process. Eventually, you will be able to apply these upgrades 'on the fly' while a negative event is in progress, and you will be able to see an alternative reality of what is happening. You will find you can deal with situations as they arrive and not feel as stressed or anxious.

I have been actively practising this technique for a couple of years and I am glad to say that for the most part, I live in the upgraded acceptance state. If you can persist with looking for the positives and eliminating the WISH mentality, life will look a lot brighter.

I am not saying that we shouldn't feel any adverse emotions; that would be bullshit. We should allow ourselves to feel fully whatever emotion arises, but for only for a few minutes and then return to the positives. My wife and kids regularly push my buttons, as only loved ones know how to do best, but I am getting better every day at returning to the positives.

Improve your regular thoughts and words.

Keep working to improve the quality of your beliefs, thoughts and vocabulary. This will greatly improve your mental state and the health of your relationships. We have already covered beliefs relating to stress. Here I want to talk about other aspects of thoughts, words and beliefs to improve the quality of your life.

Be super vigilant of the thoughts and words you use, both in your head and spoken verbally. Be mindful throughout the day of what you think and say on a regular basis, maybe even write down your commonly repeated words and phrases. The quality and nature of your thoughts and words have such a powerful effect on your life in almost every aspect.

Remember, your brain is a biological super computer; it is hardware. The thoughts and words we speak are the outputs from the belief software. If thoughts and words come out that are constantly negative or derogatory, then your brain automatically processes that to re-enforce the incorrect beliefs.

Basix 4: Food

Did you ever watch Sesame Street as a kid or as a parent? Well up until 2014, I related very well with Cookie Monster. OMM NOM NOM NOM. I was out of control around junk food. At the worst of my depression, one night after a typical dinner, I smashed a large bag of potato chips, a whole bag of lollies, a box of Shapes biscuits and I still felt hungry! WTF?! It was a vicious cycle. The more sugar and carbs I ate, the hungrier I felt. No wonder my weight topped out at 141 kg.

I was a food addict. The problem with a food addiction is you cannot go cold turkey to get over the addiction—you still need to eat.

In the three weeks at Palladium Private™, I lost 16 kg by eating correctly, exercising and de-stressing. Since then I have lost another 11 kg. I am still around 114 kg, but my muscle mass has increased dramatically in that time. My goal weight is 100 kg—14 kg to go, but relative to 2014, I look and feel great!

Right about now I am going to rubbish the shit out of the BMI scale (Body Mass Index). It is complete crap! Currently, at 114 kg and 188cm tall, my BMI is 32—labelled OBESE. For my height and gender, my doctor recommended that my weight range is 65-88 kg.

I can tell you that this is impossible for me to achieve.

Barring illness or ailment, I have not been less than 88 kg since I was 11 years old. The BMI scale gives no consideration to genetics, frame, muscle composition or bone density. How you FEEL is more important. Feeling strong, energised and healthy is a much better gauge of health. I could also be 114 kg and mostly fat and look awful, or I could be 114 kg and mostly muscle—big difference.

So, I say fuck the numbers.

If being overweight is a problem for you, this new way of life encourages a positive re-enforcing cycle. If you eat correctly, exercise and de-stress; you will lose weight, and your hormones and endorphins—the natural happy drugs—are improved. As a result, you lose more weight and feel great. You look better, you feel better about yourself, and that re-enforces this way of living. It works!

If weight isn't an issue for you (lucky bugger), then what this way of living will do for you is get your body chemistry right. Correcting your body chemistry, hormone and endorphin levels with good food, exercise and de-stressing, should lead to you feeling happier, healthier and more energetic.

Regardless of your weight or mental state, you must remember this:

Your body is the most sophisticated machine known to mankind!

Can we replicate a human body? Heck no! It is way too complicated, WAY more complicated than an F1 racing car or fighter jet! Would you go ahead use crude oil to power those? No, only a highly refined and precise fuel mixture is used. Your body and mind also need the right fuel to perform optimally. Put in the wrong foods (think crude oil—it helps when buying that bucket of chips or deep fried chicken to think of sludge) and your health and mental state suffers! VERY simple.

If, after reading all of this, you think 'that's crap' or 'that will never work for me', then give it a go and prove me wrong! Decide and commit 100% to just three weeks of eating this way. If you still don't find any benefit, give up, but I can guarantee that you will feel a LOT better for it.

Before changing your way of eating, go to your doctor and get a full blood analysis done to give you a starting point. It also gives your doctor a chance to see if there is any underlying conditions or ailments. Be careful though if they start prescribing medications or supplements. Read up on them first—the ailment itself and the medication and any associated side effects. Chances are you have been in that condition for some time; a positive change of diet usually helps most problems. A couple of months after the diet change, get your blood tested again to make sure everything is good.

The word diet—I hate it. The following is not a diet, some people may call it a 'Way of Eating' (WOE); but it is really a 'Way of Living' (WOL). I say that because it is not just food, but also exercise and stress management. It is about eating the right foods until you feel full—not calorie counting and not starving yourself.

My recommendations for food

The following is what has worked for me. Everyone is different, so research and experiment to find what works for you. Keep getting check-ups from your healthcare provider to make sure all is well. If you object to my methods because you have different beliefs then that is fine, but I don't want to hear about it, because the proof is in my shrinking pudding—AKA waistline.

I encourage you to look into food thoroughly, don't just take my word for it. It's your life and your decision, own it and take responsibility for it, embrace it and love it, whatever your choice may be. If something is not working, research the issue (not losing weight, tiredness, whatever the ailment), ask for help, make a small change and adapt until you find what does work for you.

Avoid processed foods

Avoid any food that comes in a packet or is processed in any way. It's in a packet for a reason; to make it last as long as un-naturally possible, and more often than not loaded with preservatives, sugar, sweeteners and toxins. 2000 years ago, how much of the average diet do you think came in a packet? We evolved on natural foods, so whenever possible, stick with natural foods.

Avoid sugar

Sugar lights up the brain just like cocaine. It is super addictive, messes with your insulin levels and is a fast track to hunger, weight gain, depression, diabetes and cancer. If you are trying to lose weight, watch your consumption of natural sugars in fruits like apples, oranges and grapes, etc., as fructose has the same effect. If you want something sweet, get stuck into the berries: strawberries, blueberries, mulberries, cranberries; basically, any berry. Berries are lower in sugar and contain many other goodies like antioxidants, vitamins, etc.

Avoid artificial sweeteners

Mostly these are toxic; do the research, there is plenty of evidence. If it's not artificial (honey, agave, maple syrup) it's usually high in sugar. Some say stevia is OK, but there are not enough studies done on this. In my opinion, artificial sweeteners = artificial health.

Avoid grains

Avoid all grains including corn and rice; they are hard for a reason—they are not meant to be eaten, with or without processing or cooking. Wheat products are highly addictive and trigger over-eating. A majority of the population is gluten intolerant without even knowing it or realising the effects. Grain products are usually high in carbohydrates, effectively converted by the body into glucose—see sugar above—messing with insulin levels and triggering weight gain.

I personally have a very high inflammation response to almost all grains. A day or two after eating them, I almost always get a sore back and joints.

Avoid 'gluten free' processed products
Quite often the 'gluten-free' substitutes can be just as bad for you. Safest thing is to avoid all packet/processed foods. Keep it natural.

Avoid starchy foods
Avoid starchy foods like potato and rice. Mixed with fats (e.g. French fries) these mess with insulin levels and hamper weight loss. Sweet potato and pumpkin are much better, but still not great when mixed with fats.

Reduce salt intake
It makes you thirsty, retain fluids, and raises blood pressure.

Avoid bad fats
Anything processed or heat-treated (damaged fats) like vegetable oils, canola/rapeseed oils (very unstable when heated—turns rancid) and margarine. Especially avoid fast food that is deep fried in used and re-used oils. Bad fats or hydrogenated oils, also known as 'trans fats', are the ones that cause the problems.

Eat more of the good fats
By good fats, I mean fats that occur naturally in food. This includes fish oil, avocado, coconut oil, (grass fed) butter, (grass fed) meats and nuts. Fats have had a bad rap. Low-fat diets have been 'the norm' for so long thanks to 'professionals' touting

that fat increases your risk of heart disease, cholesterol, etc. It's outright bullshit. We NEED good fats. It helps to regulate insulin and satiates hunger (makes you feel full). Contrary to popular beliefs, eating good fats helps weight loss.

Meats

Meats (preferably grass fed—higher in Omega 3's) are a source of good fats and protein. If you eat too much protein, your body, an elaborate chemistry set, converts excess protein into glucose (see sugars above) and a host of other issues. Typically, your protein intake should aim at 10–20% of your caloric intake. Protein toxicity (and other adverse effects) begins at around 230 grams a day. I typically aim at around 100 grams of protein a day (but I am a large male). This one I struggle with even now, as I love my meat.

Water

Drink two or three BIG glasses of water (1 to 1.5 litres) first thing in the morning (preferably fresh/rain/filtered/unchlorinated). Prepare yourself to go to the toilet because this tends to get things moving, but it also gets you pre-hydrated for the day ahead, not to mention expelling a bunch of waste and toxins. It also helps you to feel less hungry. Drink another 6–8 glasses throughout the rest of the day (more if physically exerting). If you are thirsty, you are already dehydrated or being manipulated by salt.

Alcohol

Alcohol effectively gets broken down by the body into glucose/

sugar (see sugar above). It is also a depressant. If you must drink, try to limit consumption to 0 to 1 glasses a day. Preferably red wine (has some beneficial aspects), or if spirits are your choice of poison (yes, alcohol is poison—Methylated spirits and rubbing alcohol bottles are labelled 'poison' for a reason) use low sugar mixers or even better—on the rocks.

Caution on dairy

I personally avoid all dairy as I get a bad phlegm response to it. Another reason is that for the equivalent G.I. rating, dairy has a very high insulinemic response (increases insulin response) compared to other foods. Meaning it would have a similar effect to sugar. If you find you have adverse reactions to dairy, try cut it out entirely for a few weeks and see how you go.

Slow the Funk down!

When you eat, slow down and chew your food more. Savour the flavours of the good foods. It is better for the digestive system and gives your body and brain time to send and receive the 'full' signal.

Supplements

Our over-farmed soils are heavily depleted of trace minerals. Trace minerals are those that are normally absorbed by our natural foods when they grow. As a result, our bodies are not getting the trace minerals they need, especially magnesium. I take concentrated trace mineral tablets that contain 72 trace minerals. I also take fish oil tablets for extra Omega 3.

All calories are not created equal

Forget calorie counting! If you eat the right foods, you eat until you feel full. But slow down, it takes time for the body to signal your brain that it is full.

Snacks

If you get hungry, eat. But eat the right foods as discussed here. My personal favourites to snack on are celery and carrots which are cheap, high in fibre, high in water content, filling and low carb. Also, nut mix has good fats—my favourite is a blend of cashews, almonds, pistachios, macadamias and dried cranberries (for some sweetness)—but be careful, nut mix is nutrient dense and is easy to over-eat.

Stay 'on the wagon'

When, not if, you 'fall off the wagon' and eat things that you 'shouldn't', don't beat yourself up—everyone slips. Take notice of any adverse effects that show up such as weight gain, gut pain, feeling lethargic or sleepy, feeling depressed for no logical reason, or feeling sick. Take note of these adverse effects, and remember these for next time you might slip. I fell off the wagon recently and it ran over me—I put on 8 kg in two days. Fortunately, returning to this way of eating, that weight came off again in four days, but it was a good reminder to stay the course.

Remove the temptations

I find the best way to avoid the wrong foods is to remove them entirely from my environment. This can be a challenge when going to parties or someone else's house. Let them know beforehand or take some of your own foods/snacks.

Last thoughts

Eating healthy is HARD! Why?

- Because of the abundance and easy availability of processed/artificial foods vs healthy and natural food.
- Because processed/artificial food is relatively cheap. Not in the long run—what value can you put on your health and life?
- Because processed or artificial foods taste good and are super addictive. You have a history with food that is hard to avoid.
- Because most other people eat a lot of processed foods. When you go to someone else's house or a function they will more than likely serve up conventional processed foods.

As mentioned above, there will be times when you slip. Don't be hard on yourself. Accept it and return. Don't get sucked into the idea that you're off the wagon, you might as well binge on shit food.

My parting words on this topic are simple. What can be more natural than eating natural food? It's what we, as a species, have evolved on, not this processed and artificial crap that has shown up in the last century or so.

Basix 5: Exercise

Ever since I was a little boy, I have hated running. It must be genetics. Some people are born runners, I am not one of them. It makes my lungs burn, head throb and everything ache. As a result, I grew up playing sports that needed less running to play the game. I dropped Aussie Rules football because it felt like you were eternally running around a paddock—just too much hard work. Instead, I took up grass hockey which had a much smaller field and a LOT less running. Having a smaller field also felt like I was a bigger part of the game, with increased interaction with the gameplay.

My sport of choice now is squash. Who would have thought you could get so tired running around such a small space after a little black ball? I prefer the short burst running, but it is also a tactical game, almost like mobile chess. You need to think a couple of moves ahead to get the better of your opponent. You can also belt the shit out of the ball, and it normally stays in play, unlike tennis, where you need finesse to keep it in— besides, smashing the little black ball can be quite therapeutic.

Exercise is equally as important to your overall health as the other Basix. Most importantly, it gets the endorphins going— the natural happy drugs. Simply put, exercise helps you feel better, healthier and happier. Remember this:

Do not exercise to lose weight. Food is for the body, Exercise is for the head.

Losing weight is 80% diet and 20% exercise. Do you know how many hours you would have to run to burn off a Big Mac? Too many! It is much easier to eat well than exercise eternally.

Other benefits of exercise:
- Improves health conditions such as high blood pressure, heart disease, metabolic syndrome, stroke, diabetes, some cancers, arthritis, etc.
- Boosts energy. Feel lethargic or tired? Go for a brisk walk. Let me know how you feel afterwards. Repeated exercise also helps to improve energy levels in general.
- Better sleep. After exercise, your body needs to recover and repair. Falling asleep becomes easier, and the quality of sleep is also improved. Just don't exercise too close to bedtime because you may be too awake or energised.
- Can be a lot of fun. Find what works for you.
- Team sports have the added benefit of social interaction and team building.
- Improves libido—enough said.

For me, running is evil, but I enjoy playing sports. I have found that if it is fun, I enjoy exercise. If it is boring, or too painful, I avoid it like the plague.

Body By Science

An excellent resource on exercise is a book titled *Body by Science* by John Little and Doug McGuff. I strongly suggest buying the book, I have found it VERY effective. In essence:
- You do one or two workouts a week that take 12–15 minutes

each.

- Each 12–15 minute workout consists of 5 exercises, done preferably on machines (rather than free-weights. This is for motion control under muscle fatigue/failure). The five beginning exercises are:
  - o Seated row – back and rear of shoulders.
  - o Bench press – front of shoulders, triceps and chest.
  - o Seated pull-down (in front, hands shoulder width) – biceps,   abs, lats.
  - o Inclined press – front and tops of shoulders, triceps, traps.
  - o Leg press – most of legs and buttocks.
- Each of these exercises is a compound movement that works multiple muscle groups all at the same time.
- First, you find out what the maximum possible weight is that you can move (with good form) for each exercise. Then do the exercise, setting the working weight to about 75% of maximum weight. Each movement should be very slow and controlled. The slower the better.
- Each exercise should last 60–90 seconds until you are completely exhausted (cannot move the weight at all whilst maintaining form). Once you hit 'failure' and cannot move the weight, you hold the weight for another 10–15 seconds to extend the benefits. If you get to failure before 60 seconds the weight is too heavy; next time drop the weight 5–10%. If you can keep powering past 90 seconds the weight is too light; next time increase the weight by 5–10%. Eventually, you will find the correct weight to start with.

- The idea is that in the 60–90 seconds you completely burn the glycogen (energy) stores in your muscles.
- Don't waste time between the exercises. Finish one, start the next ASAP.

By the end of it, you will be blowing HARD, and you may feel like passing out. Don't stress, as this is fairly normal. The workout is INTENSE. Avoid highly strenuous and lengthy exercises like running. The high shock loading to your body's joints will increase wear and tear and increase the likelihood of injury.

I love the 'Body by Science' workout. OK, granted, I hate going to the gym. I also hate the boring act of lifting or moving weights. BUT it only takes 12–15 minutes once or twice a week to get buggered to exhaustion. Doing 'Body by Science', my weight loss has slowed down, but my muscle mass has greatly increased meaning my physique has changed. I used to have ski-jump moobs (man-boobs), now I feel like I have a muscular, manly, and somewhat toned chest. I feel good about how I look, even though I haven't lost as much weight as I would like. I feel strong, and I feel powerful, AND it's easy to find 15 minutes to exercise!

Other exercises

Lately, I have been trying an alternative which is working quite well. Every morning I roll out of bed and plop down on the floor. I do 20 slow and full stroke push-ups—nose to floor, up to arms straight; 50 crunches; 20 slow and controlled leg raises; then 50 hip raises for my lower back. All this only takes 10–15 minutes. The point here is not the type of exercise or the quantity, but the habit and convenience of it. Every morning it is part of my routine, no matter where I am, and no matter what my time constraints. I can always find 10–15 minutes, so there is no excuse not to do it.

If there are areas of your body that you either want to strengthen or change shape, find the appropriate body weight exercise that will achieve your desired outcomes and do those. When starting out it is VERY important to make it so easy that it seems silly not to do it. This helps to develop the regular habit as part of your daily routine. Once the routine or habit is well established then start to ramp up the intensity.

If you can't find 15 minutes to exercise, I call bullshit—you are lying to yourself. There are 1440 minutes in every day, so do yourself a REAL favour and 'Just do it'. If you can't afford to go to the gym, then improvise with body weight exercises. Decide and commit 100%.

I like to move my body every day, just to get the endorphins going. I find it most pleasant to go for a half-hour walk early in the morning around sunrise. Some mornings the sunrise is just magic. The sun comes up and beams through the cloud cover giving spectacular colours. To me, it's like viewing nature's art exhibition. It is also interesting going for a walk and being mindful of my thoughts, paying attention to what comes up or is persistent in my mind (then apply 'What's in the way, is the way').

Other great forms of exercise include yoga, rock climbing, Pilates, riding a bike, swimming and so much more. Google ideas and find what works for you. Find something you enjoy, because if you enjoy it, it's not a chore, it's a pleasure. It's good to get the heart going, get the blood pumping and feel alive.

Tip for the single men … if you want to meet fit attractive ladies, try Pilates, yoga, etc., as they offer a bloody good workout with some very nice scenery.

To finish off this section, the saying which comes to mind, and something that I find very true:

'Use it or lose it', meaning use your body, or lose your health, both physical and mental.

Basix 6: Peace of Mind

What is this Peace of Mind (POM) stuff? It's last on the list of the Basix; it mustn't be that important, right?

Wrong! Peace of Mind is one of the more important elements of the Basix. But why? Because POM has a symbiotic relationship with each of the other Basix—the other five aid POM, and in turn POM helps to drive the other five Basix.

First, let's define Peace of Mind. It is:
• The opposite of feeling stressed.
• The ability to turn off the chatter in your head, on command.
• The clarity to make better decisions under pressure.
• The ability to pause between action and reaction.
• The ability to be present in the moment without distraction.
• Mental toughness.
• Being OK with who you are and your past.
• The glue that holds the rest of the Basix together.

How do the other Basix affect POM?
• Choice, Decision and Commitment. Deciding with 100% commitment takes a load off the mind, as it stops the worrying and stress about procrastination and following through. 100% commitment is a breeze!
• Goals, Habits and Growth. Goals give direction and hope. Having a solid set of habits takes very little brainpower or willpower to execute as you do them automatically. Growth and learning help to exercise the brain, keeping it sharp.

- Thoughts and Beliefs. Identifying shitty beliefs and upgrading to shit-hot beliefs helps to reduce your stress. You take a load off the mind by addressing your beliefs and feeling more calm, with a more positive outlook on life.
- Food. The correct fuel ensures the brain is performing optimally which aids peace of mind. Think of a three-year-old child hopped up on sugar—the opposite of POM.
- Exercise. Stimulates the release of endorphins and reduces cortisol, building muscle, feeling strong and powerful, looking better and feeling better about yourself, all aid POM.

Without POM, the other Basix suffer, making it difficult to focus and to think correctly about them, to keep the quality or quantity up, or to follow through.

Now let's look at ways to build Peace of Mind.

Sleep

Possibly the most important factor, good quality sleep is critical for peace of mind. Everyone is different, but try to get a regular 7 to 10 hours of good quality sleep every night. For a couple of weeks, try waking up without an alarm and see how long you naturally sleep to feel refreshed in the morning. Plan your time into bed and time to sleep to coincide with the time you need to wake up and still achieve your ideal 7 to 10 hours. Ensure the room is dark and try to remove any lights that shine on your eyes. Try to eliminate screen time just before sleep. Read a book, but nothing too thought provoking.

If you still fail to feel refreshed first thing in the morning, no matter how long you sleep, I would strongly recommend getting tested for sleep apnoea or other sleep disorders.

Get adequate rest

Along with adequate sleep, ensure you have enough quality rest periods between work. If you work a conventional five days a week job, use one of your days off to smash out all of the odd jobs and social outings, and the other day just rest and do what it is that you want to do. Preferably something constructive that aids in personal growth, but slow, easy and relaxed: read, learn something of interest, do a creative hobby, relax with friends, listen to music, have some fun.

Throughout your workdays, if you find yourself procrastinating a lot, it is often a sign that you have not had sufficient rest. Step away and take 10 minutes for yourself to either meditate, power-nap or take a quick walk. Try to do this at least every 2 hours of time worked. When you return, you will be able to focus better and be more productive. Go hard at it while you can and then when your focus wanes, step away for a quick rest.

Be kind to yourself

Often, we treat ourselves harshly or speak to ourselves degradingly, and think little of ourselves. If we treated others the way we treat ourselves, we would probably be locked up in jail—that has to stop!

Treat yourself the way you would treat your most cherished

family members or friends—be gentle, caring and forgiving towards yourself. Build yourself up rather than tear yourself down.

Stop 'time travelling'

In the 'My Journey' chapter at the beginning of the book, there are three big sliding doors moments that I have highlighted. If you haven't seen the movie 'Sliding Doors' starring Gwyneth Paltrow, a sliding doors moment is a point in your past, or present, where you face a massive choice, and where the outcomes of that choice can spin your life off in drastically different directions.

For so long I dwelled on those moments and pondered what could have been. For many years after leaving Kristy, I WISHed that I could go back in time and take the other path. This thought caused me a lot of stress and ultimately depression.

These days, after applying the shit-hot upgrades, I am so grateful to have had all of those experiences because that has led to this point now, where I have a fantastic wife and two amazing kids. I have experiences that I can draw upon to help others, I am feeling and looking better every day, and my learning curve has taken off once again; I am so thankful for all of it! Without my past, I would not be where I am today, and for me that is a good place to be.

Sometimes it can be pleasant to go back and ponder what if, but more often than not, if WISHing comes into it, then that pondering on the past is acting as an anchor, dragging you down.

Let yourself be OK with your past, no matter what has been done. The past is gone and cannot be changed, and the future will never happen the way you want it to, for better or worse.

Some interesting thoughts on staying present:
- Depression is living in the past.
- Anxiety is living in the future.
- You cannot be in both states of anxiety and depression at the same time.
- You may flip flop between the two instantly, but it is impossible to be in both states at once.

If you are in the present, you cannot be in the future or the past. If you are present, you cannot be in a state of worry, anxiety or depression. So stop time travelling.

I have always suffered from social anxiety. I think the main worries that I used to have was 'What are they thinking of me?' or 'Do they like me?' or 'I hope I am not making a fool of myself'. Just a couple of months ago, I had my 20-year high school reunion. In the time leading up to that date, I didn't think about it much, but on the drive to the event, I could feel those old tendencies creeping up, and I admit I felt somewhat anxious. That was, until I had the thought, *'I didn't have these people in my life yesterday, most of them won't be in my life tomorrow, so fuck it, I am going to enjoy the shit out of tonight.'* And you know what? I had a blast. I felt like a bit of a dill-pickle after knocking over a couple of drinks, but you know what? Shit happens. I strongly recommend remembering that concept:

I didn't have them yesterday, I probably won't have them tomorrow, so I am going to enjoy myself right now.

It has worked wonders for me.

Meditation

Many years ago, if you told me to meditate, I would have laughed at you, if not mentally bitch-slapped you. I was a very conventional thinker in most aspects of life. 'Me? Meditate? Pfft ... forget it!'

Look where that got me—depressed and suicidal.

Well, if you can get past that initial resistance, or the 'lah-dee-dah hippy-shit' conventional stigma, give it a try. Meditation is a VERY powerful tool to quiet the mind, build mental toughness and stay present. Remember this saying:

Meditation is to the mind what exercise is to the muscles.

It is how you work out to achieve Peace of Mind. Here is a list of some benefits of meditating:
- Improves relaxation and stress reduction.
- Help to stay present throughout your day.
- Improves relationships and connections with others.
- Helps you appreciate life more.

- Reduces the effects of stress-related ageing.
- Helps with a better night's sleep.
- Improves brain function.
- Improves focus, clarity, and attention span.
- Helps the immune system.
- Improves mood and behaviour.
- Helps cut through the bullshit of life.

Meditation is more than just shutting your eyes and sitting quietly. Essentially, all meditations boil down to focusing your attention on a single sensation, mantra or concept. If your focus wanders off, smile and acknowledge the thought, and return to your focal point. I have heard it said that the point of meditation is not just to stay focused, but to keep bringing yourself back to focus. Each time that you bring yourself back to the point of focus, think of that as one mental push-up.

There are so many forms, variations and combinations of meditation. The trick is finding what works best for you. Here is a list of the most popular kinds of meditations:

- Transcendental Meditation (TM), which typically focuses on a mantra.
- Mindfulness, which typically focuses on sensations.
- Holosync or paraliminals or audio brainwave entrainment where you listen to special audio tracks to help alter brain wave patterns. This can be used in combination with other meditations for better effect.
- Guided meditations. Search YouTube for 'guided meditation'

and you'll find many that are free.

Here is one of the simplest meditations that anyone can perform, at any time. Follow these steps:

- Sit up in a comfortable position that requires little effort to stay upright, or lay down.
- Close your eyes.
- Take several very deep breaths in and out.
- On each deep exhale, try to relax all of your body, let go of any muscular tension.
- Relax back to your normal comfortable breathing.
- Let your belly relax.
- Focus constantly on the sensation of the fresh air passing through your nostrils or mouth as you breathe.
- If any thought, sensation or muscle tension or discomfort comes up, smile, acknowledge it, let it go, and return your focus to the sensation of the breath. Don't be hard on yourself if you get distracted, gently return your focus.
- Do this for a set time, preferably with a gentle alarm and a timer.

There is no such thing as a good or bad meditation session. There will be days when it is easier to focus than others. This is normal, so don't be hard on yourself. Smile and return.

Start off with short sessions so you are more likely to stick with it.

In time, do more research into the other forms of meditation.

Try them out and find what works best for you. Everyone is different.

Decide and commit yourself 100% to it for 30 days. It is not a huge investment—5 to 10 minutes a day (out of 1440 minutes in a day, 5 to 10 minutes is fuck all), but the possible benefits are massive. Try the simple meditation above. If after 30 days you don't feel any benefit at all, then flag it and go back to not doing it, but I think you will feel quite a difference.

Another interesting observation I have is that a common theme between big name entrepreneurs in '30 days of genius' with Chase Jarvis, was that many of them meditated as part of their daily routine and swear by it.

Grip it and rip it

Let yourself feel any emotion, with great intensity, for only 90 seconds, then choose to shift your focus. Remember that where your focus is where you go. If you keep dwelling on the negative or sad you will spiral into depression. Look for positives and lift yourself once you are done.

Stuff, clutter and minimalism

A house or workspace full of clutter is detrimental to Peace of Mind. Your eyes work overtime as you scan the area, and with so many objects your mind goes into overdrive.

If possible, keep your working and living areas clear of clutter.

Have some fun

Find what you enjoy doing and have some fun. What is the point of life if you can't enjoy the journey? As the saying goes, 'All work and no play makes Johnny a dull boy.' Check out Meetup.com for activities and groups that interest you in your area, join a club that interests you, or whatever floats your boat, but enjoyment is doubled if it is shared with others.

Live a Better Life

This chapter contains additional information on top of the Basix that also help to live a better life. These are separate of the Basix, as they are not critical to their effectiveness, but additive in nature and well worth a mention.

Write yourself a new code of conduct

You have your Basix under way, your goals are in-line, and you have formed habits to reach your goals—great! Now what?

Well, live life day by day, but a better version of life, because your old ways weren't working. Write yourself a new code of conduct and hold yourself to a higher standard, but without being hard on yourself.

> *"Any time you sincerely want to make a change, the first thing you must do is raise your standards."*
>
> Tony Robbins

Keep checking yourself constantly

Remember the mind-body connection? Check yourself constantly. Everything may 'feel' OK, but monitor the sensations in your body. I know when I am stressed or worried about something; I feel a very distinct tension in my gut. It is these signals that we need to monitor constantly. When you do notice that you are feeling something physically, ask yourself the question, 'What am I thinking, to feel this way?' Then address those thoughts or events by checking the beliefs behind the thoughts or reactions, and then address those by upgrading the shitty beliefs (refer to Basix 3) and reduce your stress via meditation or exercise.

Keep checking! Keep working on the driving beliefs.

Additional treatments

Building your Basix will help to change your life, but the process is long and gradual. If you are in a real hurry to get to the bottom of things and want to 'nip it in the bud' quickly, then you may need help to do so.

Keep trying until you find what works for you. Keep an open mind with any new treatment. Treat yourself as a science experiment, observe and record how you feel prior to, during and after each treatment. If you go in with a 'this won't work' attitude, you know how you're going to come out, right? An open mind makes change possible.

<u>Conventional Medicine</u>

If you seek immediate help from your conventional GP, doctor, psychologist, psychiatrist, hospital, etc., generally speaking, they will put you through fairly conventional treatment methods. In my opinion, some of these can be good to a point, but often they will prescribe medications to help with the symptoms. Meds may help immediately by masking the symptoms, but they don't heal the root cause of your stress, anxiety, depression or other issues. With any diagnosis and prescription, do your research and check into the possible side effects (some can be pretty nasty) before taking any meds and look for possible alternatives. I am not saying don't take the medications or treatments, just be happy with YOUR decision of what YOU are putting into YOUR body first. Medications are ultimately man-made, highly processed chemicals designed to alter your natural body chemistry.

It may be necessary to medicate if diagnosed with serious mental conditions like bipolar disorder, schizophrenia, etc. Regardless, it is imperative that you still work HARD on the Basix: Decisions, Habits, Beliefs, Food, Exercise, and Peace of Mind. In many cases, this alone may reduce or eliminate the need for those meds. Don't let any 'diagnosis' be an excuse for not working hard on your Basix. My point here is this; work closely with your prescribing physician with the end goal of minimising or eliminating your meds.

Journey Therapy

My favourite treatment at Palladium Private™ was an adaptation of Journey Therapy (JT) which they called 'Discovery Therapy'(DT). Here's a definition of conventional Journey Therapy, taken from www.goodtherapy.org to give you some context:

Journey Therapy is a process by which a person is guided to uncover suppressed memories that are responsible for creating problematic issues in the present day. By doing this, a person is liberated from the emotion that is tied to that memory. Healing begins when the negative emotion is released. In Journey Therapy, the therapist works with the client without direct physical contact, to supply him or her with the tools necessary to discover the memories within. Once this is achieved, the behaviours associated with the memories are identified and studied. The therapist and client work together to determine which patterns must be altered in order to affect a positive change in the person's life, health, and relationships.'

In my Discovery Therapy sessions, the two major things that came up for me were:

• Missing my mum.
• Grieving the loss of my Pa.

There were other things too, but these two really blindsided me as to their severity. Through discovery therapy, we were quickly able to reduce the severity and intensity of the emotion that I felt about those things. I found it quite amazing, almost like turning a light switch off.

I am not saying Discovery Therapy or Journey Therapy will work for everyone, but it may be worth a shot. If you find it doesn't work in one or two sessions, try another therapist. Try several. Like any profession, competence, talent and expertise levels will vary.

Massage

Another therapy that I have adopted long-term is regular massage. In my opinion, remedial massage is best, but these days I have a deep tissue massage once a week for 90 minutes as my reward for working hard. It is a good way to remove tension in the body, and it's 90 minutes to relax and let the mind wander. It feels great, which helps me feel great! It doesn't necessarily help with any root cause issues, but it sure helps the physical release of tension, and allows me to relax and de-stress. Just like any therapist, keep trying until you find one that works for you.

Chiropractic Treatment

I have a history of back problems which occasionally still pops up. Even though I am stronger than ever, I sometimes move or lift the wrong way which can exacerbate my back, and I turn into a bit of a grumpy bastard. So, off to the chiro I go to get 'straightened out'. Now this therapy for me is not directly related to the Basix, but if my back is out, my Basix suffer. Consequently, I use chiropractic treatment as a maintenance tool.

Other Therapies

Possibly try other therapies that focus on dealing with the root causes of your symptoms:
- Emotional Freedom Techniques (EFT), often known as tapping.
- Acupuncture.
- Neuro Linguistic Programming (NLP).
- Hypnotherapy.
- Cognitive Behavioural Therapy (CBT).
- Kinesiology.

They may be worth a try. Do your research!

Social life

I have always been a bit of a loner and an introvert. Maybe it was all the moving around as a child, maybe it was a fear of loss or abandonment. I used to blame others for the way I was, and I used to hate being different. Why? Because society says you need to have lots of friends? Do you need to be popular?

Now, you know what? I don't care. I am who I am, and I am OK with that, 100%.

An interesting saying comes to mind. '1 in 3 people will love you, 1 in 3 will hate you and 1 in 3 won't give a shit', meaning that 2 out of 3 people won't give a shit about you, or worse. That is OK, that's life. Focus on the 1 in 3 that love you, and put your effort into those people.

If you feel good within yourself and about yourself, you don't NEED anyone else to validate your existence.

However, I do feel it is important to have a few very good friends in your life. I take quality over quantity every time. If you have 500 Facebook friends, does that make you popular or happy? I don't think so. Real connection with others is what makes life truly interesting, sharing experiences and making memories together.

The most important factor when it comes to friends, is choosing them wisely, especially if your past is sketchy. The saying goes, 'You are the average of your five closest friends'. Look at the five closest friends that you spend most of your time with. How do they make you feel? Are they people that you truly like, admire, and want to be like? If not, maybe it's time to put some distance between you, especially if they partake in or offer temptations that are at odds with your new goals, habits and values, such as smoking, drinking, drug taking, gossiping, etc.

Alternatively, if you look at your five closest friends, and you find one or two of them that you love dearly and want to keep as friends, but you don't like their attitudes, history or ways, then be the beacon for them. Work HARD on yourself to show them another way to live. Don't impose your thoughts and beliefs directly, as nobody likes to be told what to do, but lead by example. Ultimately, if they don't want to follow your example and it keeps adversely affecting your life, cut your ties and hold yourself to a higher standard. YOU are the one who determines what is and is not acceptable to YOU.

If you want to make new, 'better quality' friends, do things that you truly love and aspire to do, but do it around other people. Join a club, join a committee, volunteer for a worthy cause, check out Meetup.com for interesting groups in your local area. Through these ventures you will meet people with similar interests, so step out of your comfort zone, and if you find someone you admire, talk to them. It's a good start.

If you have or manage to build a solid friendship, work HARD at keeping that relationship healthy. Go out of your way to make time and effort for those five closest to you. Life is about increasing returns, the more effort you put into other people the more effort people will put into you.

Quick Review

The following is a quick summary of the takeaways intended for each section. If you skipped straight to this section that is fine, but please don't take any of the following lightly, as this is the essence of golden information that has changed my life, and if applied, will do for you too. If there is something that doesn't make sense, refer back to the equivalent chapter. Use this as a quick reference to remind you from time to time what is important.

Introduction

Hold on to hope that life can be great once again. Make the decision for change and use this book as a guide to find what works for you, and don't give up until you find your solution.

If YOU want change in YOUR life, it is YOU who needs to make that change happen.

Back to Basix

Often the solutions come from within, and one of the most powerful methods to reduce stress, depression and anxiety is to get back to Basix:

1. Choice, Decision and Commitment
2. Goals, Habits and Growth
3. Thoughts and Beliefs
4. Food
5. Exercise
6. Peace of Mind.

You may do some of these Basix well already, but ALL six need to be of equal strength to achieve a balanced and healthy life.

Basix 1: Choice, Decision and Commitment

The solutions come from within; they start with a choice, are possible with a decision and happen with absolute commitment.

Choice: Essentially, all choices come down to this: Keep doing what I am doing (the safe road) or get out of my comfort zone and face the fear of making the change.

Decision: A decision without a commitment is merely a hope.

Commitment: '99% commitment is a bitch, 100% is a breeze'. True commitment makes it easy to follow through to completion.

Ask better quality questions to make better quality decisions. Five shit-hot questions to constantly be asking:

1. What is the better question I could be asking?
2. On my deathbed, what option would make me most proud?
3. What advice would I give to my child if they were in the same situation?
4. What is it that I REALLY want?
5. What are my other options?

Fear: Use fear as a guide rather than a deterrent. Step toward the fear.

What's in the way is the way: If something is bothering you, deal with it before it has a chance to escalate.

Integrity: Without it you don't have shit—live with honesty and integrity.

What is the next step? And just keep chewing. Instead of setting and following a rigid plan, always ask, 'What is the next step?', then DO it. Then ask again, and DO it. Repeat until you succeed. In cases where you feel overwhelmed, remember the saying:

'If you have a plateful to get through, just keep chewing. Otherwise you will choke.'

Basix 2: Goals, Habits and Growth

Growth: If you are not growing, you are decaying. Learn and try new things every day. It gives variety and who knows you may stumble upon your purpose.

Goals: Specific, Measurable, Achievable, Realistic, Time based (SMART) goals are great to give you direction and motivation. Never attach your self-worth to goals, and only set goals for yourself, not for the desires of others. It is OK to fail at goals, just re-assess, re-commit and retry.

Habits: For any goal that you wish to achieve, find and form the regular habits to support those goals. Forming a regular habit makes it easier to succeed, because once a habit is formed the behaviour for progress becomes automatic or routine. When initially forming any habit, make it so easy that you can't not do it.

1% Rule: Once the habit is formed and becomes automatic, then ramp up the outputs 1% every time. Make the increase so small it is almost negligible, with compounding over a year, the difference becomes massive.

Failure: Embrace it, learn from it, grow from it, accept it. It is a natural part of life, and the best way to learn valuable lessons.

Recommended habits to develop:
- Daily Routine.
- Exercise your 'Idea Muscle'—10 ideas daily practice.
- Develop an attitude of gratitude and appreciation.
- Develop mental toughness.
- Visualisation: Picture with conviction, that which you will achieve.
- Creativity: Something creative every day.
- Get some sun.

Basix 3: Thoughts and Beliefs

Wishing that something was different causes us stress. The four shitty beliefs that cause us stress:

1. Shit is not going to plan.
2. Missing out on shit.
3. Should have done shit differently.
4. I am a piece of shit.

Accepting reality helps to reduce stress. The four shit-hot upgrades:

1. **Shit does happen:** Life is a rollercoaster, take the good with the bad.

2. **I gain when I lose shit:** There is valuable learning in every situation.

3. **Did the best with the shit we had:** We always do the best we can at the time.

4. **I am always shit-hot:** I am always worthy.

Journalling an emotional or stressful event is a powerful way to express your emotion in full. Analyse the story to identify the shitty beliefs. Then re-write, upgrading the shitty beliefs with the corresponding shit-hot upgrades. Read your new story. If it still doesn't feel right, repeat the whole process until it does feel right.

When you get good at 'upgrading' you will be able to apply the shit-hot upgrades 'on the fly' as a stressful or emotional event happens.

Improve your regular thoughts and words—make note of the thoughts and words you use that don't serve you. Make a conscious effort to use better quality positive words and thoughts instead.

Basix 4: Food

Keep it clean and natural, it's how we evolved as a species, not this processed and packaged 'food' that has shown up in the last few centuries. If comes in a packet or is processed in any way don't eat it.

Avoid white foods (except cauliflower), namely sugar, flours, rice, potato.

Eat good fats that occur naturally in our food sources, not processed oils or deep fried shit.

Sources of good fats: Coconut oil, meat, butter, ghee, nuts, fish.

Avoid bad fats: Canola oil, vegetable oils, anything deep fried, margarine

I basically eat meat and vegetables and minimise fruit intake because of natural sugar (fructose). Berries are OK.

Minimise alcohol consumption: It is high in sugar and is a depressant.

Remove temptations from your environment.

When you slip-up, just return to good habits without being hard on yourself.

Basix 5: Exercise

Do not exercise to lose weight. Food is for the body, exercise is for the head. Losing weight is 80% diet and 20% exercise. Exercise for the endorphins, the natural happy drugs, that make you feel great.

Move it or lose it, meaning move your body or lose your health, both mental and physical.

Try to find 30 minutes for daily exercise daily, which can be as simple as a leisurely walk.

Read *Body by Science* by John Little and Dough McGuff, an intense weights exercise routine that takes 12–15 minutes, once or twice a week. Very effective and all backed by science.

Find a sport that you enjoy playing, preferably a team sport for the added bonus of social interaction.

Basix 6: Peace of Mind

Peace of mind is:
- The opposite of feeling stressed.
- The ability to turn off the chatter in your head, on command.
- The clarity to make better decisions under pressure.
- The ability to pause between action and reaction.
- The ability to be present in the moment without distraction.
- Mental toughness.
- Being OK with who you are and your past.
- The glue that holds the rest of the Basix together.

It has a symbiotic relationship with the other Basix. The other Basix help to build peace of mind, and alternatively, peace of mind helps to follow through with the other Basix.

The best ways to build peace of mind:

- Get enough sleep: 7–10 hours a night, enough to feel refreshed. If you wake up groggy and lethargic, chances are you aren't getting enough sleep.
- Get adequate rest: You cannot work all of your waking hours, you must take sufficient rest time each week to 'recharge the batteries'.
- Meditation or mindfulness: Train your brain to focus on a sensation or thought.
- Be kind to yourself.
- Stop time travelling and stay present in the now. Anxiety is living in the future, depression is living in the past so enjoy the shit out of now!
- Grip it and rip it: Let yourself feel any emotion fully but only for a short while. Then change your focus. Having a cry can help to relieve stress and help feel better. We have the ability to cry for a reason!
- Declutter and live a minimal life: Visual clutter and too much crap means a messy environment and a messy mind.
- Have some fun: Find shit that you love doing and make regular time to have some fun.

Live a better life

Write yourself a new code of conduct. Raise your standards and BE the person that you want to be. Set yourself rules and abide by them, ensuring that those rules are in-line with your core values.

Keep checking yourself constantly. Check your bodily sensations for any sign of stress, discomfort, or pain and address the cause immediately.

Additional treatments. Even though the Basix is a good start, sometimes anxiety and depression cannot be fixed by just the Basix alone. There are lots of other treatments out there—try them and find what works for you, but if you feel like you aren't getting any benefit, move on to the next one. Other treatments to try:

- Conventional medicine—sometimes there is a genuine chemical/hormonal imbalance or medical condition, such as bipolar disorder or schizophrenia, that need medications to correct.
- Journey Therapy or Discovery Therapy.
- Massage: A good way to relieve physical stress.
- Chiropractic treatment: Keeps the spine and nervous system functioning correctly.
- Emotional Freedom Techniques (EFT), often known as tapping.
- Acupuncture.
- Neuro Linguistic Programming (NLP).
- Hypnotherapy.
- Cognitive Behavioural Therapy (CBT).
- Kinesiology.

Keep trying until you find what works for you. An open mind makes change possible.

Social life. Friendships are important and real connection with others is what gives life meaning. You are the average of your five closest friends, so choose wisely. Choose quality over quantity and always make time for your closest friends.

Action Steps

OK, so you now have the gold nuggets of wisdom that I have found effective in my life. These took me from suicidal to happy, healthy and ambitious. As with all of the information in this book, it is what I have found effective in my life. You need to find out what is effective for you. Hopefully everything that I have written so far will be, but there are no guarantees, as we are all different. Use this as a guide or a starting place, give it a good hard honest go and if you don't find any value after three weeks, research, apply, adjust, experiment, anything … find what works for you.

If a friend of mine came to me telling me that he was depressed, sad, blue, down, in a funk, not enjoying life, feeling trapped or un-appreciated, sick of his/her life, wanting to give up, stressed, anxious, constantly sick, hating life, etc., and if I could go back in time and give myself a game plan when I felt that way, then this would be it:

1. Always, always, always hold on to hope that life can get better.

2. Realise that you are the only one who can make that happen. You may need help from other people along the way, but they can only open the door, YOU must walk through it.

3. Put yourself on a complaint ban. For the next 30 days you are not allowed to complain about anything, as focusing on the negative will send you spiralling downwards. Put an elastic

band around your wrist and every time you catch yourself complaining internally or verbally, give yourself a good hard flick with the band so that it hurts.

4. Search deep and discover what it is that you truly want. If you don't know, list down all the things that you don't want, then try find the opposite or counterpart to that. Never do this for somebody else's wants of you, only do it for yourself and your desires. Then try to reduce it to one sentence, stated in a positive way that excites you. We will call this your theme statement.

I will:
a. Live a happier, healthier, more fulfilling life (my theme statement)
b. Weigh <ideal weight>kg
c. Fit into size <ideal size> clothing
d. Feel strong, lively and energetic
e. Feel alive
f. Have great relationships
g. Be a great communicator
h. Live in <wherever>
i. Be debt free
j. Go to <event or place>
k. Do <whatever>
l. Experience <whatever>
m. Learn <whatever>
n. <whatever>

5. **Basix 1.** Decide and Commit to your theme statement. You

now have a choice you absolutely must make. Either keep doing the easy thing which has lead you to this point and keep getting the same results, or make the changes and do the hard things required to achieve your statement. Decide right now with 100% commitment to achieving that theme statement. If you feel like you cannot commit fully, then find and amplify an experience, an image, a thought, a repulsive vulgarity—anything that can convince you to commit 100%. Any image so inspiring or terrifying that you just cannot ignore, and remember that motivator, use it as fuel to flame the fire of desire to achieve your statement.

6. Write that theme statement down, or type it and print it. Then laminate it. Stick it on the wall or mirror, somewhere you will see and read it at least once a day, and when you do read it, visualise your motivating fuel image from the previous step.

7. **Basix 2.** Identify and develop the habits and a daily routine. Analyse the theme statement and what it will require to achieve, and identify any regular habits that will support the achievement of that statement. Develop a daily routine that incorporates those habits. Start off with absurdly low outputs or targets for these habits. Make it so simple it seems silly NOT to do it. The idea here is the act of setting the regular habit, not the quantity of output. Once you feel the habit is set, then start to ramp up the outputs utilising the 1% rule, increasing outputs by an average of just 1% every day. Don't try to invoke 30 habits at once, it just won't work. Work hard to focus on

invoking 1 or maybe 2 habits at one time and give that at least 2 weeks before adding more habits to your routine. If, when you add new habits, you have a time or values clash, make sure you uphold or prioritise the one habit that will benefit your theme statement the most. Also, check all of your bad habits. Identify and eliminate any that are counterproductive to your theme statement, such as too many hours of social media, TV time, mindless eating, etc.

8. **Basix 3.** Upgrade the shitty beliefs that cause you stress. Refer to Basix 3 for details on this process. Start with the events that cause you the most stress. Practice upgrading so that it becomes habit and eventually the process will become automatic.

9. **Basix 3.** Work hard to develop an attitude of gratitude and incorporate a gratitude habit into your daily routine. Do not under-estimate the power of this habit, especially when you are down. Looking up out of the hole and expressing gratitude for even the smallest good things in your life can have an uplifting effect on your mood.

10. **Basix 4.** Eat healthy natural foods. It's how we evolved as a species and our bodies need natural foods for optimal performance and body/brain chemistry. Avoid processed, treated and packaged foods. Refer to the chapter on Basix 4 for more detailed information and recommendations. What is more natural than eating natural foods?

11. **Basix 5.** Build an exercise habit into your daily routine.

Do not exercise to lose weight, only exercise to feel great. Remember 'food is for the body, exercise is for the mind'. Try to get at least 30 minutes of even the mildest exercise to get your blood pumping.

12. **Basix 6.** Ensure you get enough quality sleep every day. Everyone is different, so you need to find out how many hours you require to wake up and feel refreshed. A good way to do this is for two to three weeks, wake up without an alarm, taking note of your time to bed and your waking times to figure out sleep time and how good you feel out of 10 (10 being invincible). If you never feel refreshed, get checked for sleep apnoea or other sleeping disorders. Getting enough GOOD QUALITY sleep is essential. Once you know how many hours you need to feel refreshed in the morning, figure out what time you need to get to SLEEP to wake up at the correct time in the morning. Then ensure you GET INTO BED at least half an hour prior to sleep time. This gives the brain time to 'wind down' before sleep. Read some fiction books or non-fiction that is not too thought provoking. Then, lights out 5 minutes before sleep time.

13. **Basix 6.** Build 5–20 minutes of meditation practice into your daily routine. Meditation is to the mind, what exercise is to the muscles. Commit to doing it for 30 days and if you still feel no benefit then shit-can it. I am confident you will continue with it, as I have found this profoundly powerful in my life. Refer to Basix 6 for more detailed information on meditations.

14. Celebrate your victories! Any time you complete a challenge, goal, set a habit, or accomplish anything positive, make sure you take time to celebrate and give yourself time to enjoy that moment. DO NOT reward yourself with something that is counterproductive to your theme statement.

15. Always be asking, 'What is the next step?', then do it, repeat it, until you succeed. If you don't know how to do it, continually ask yourself, 'How can I do it?' and your brain will set about finding an answer.

Conclusion

By the end of my time at Palladium Private™ in December 2014, I had dropped 16 kg and put in a LOT of hard work to deal with my issues. I felt like a million bucks compared to a month earlier, and there was no way in hell I was going back to my old way of living. Was I apprehensive about returning home? Heck yes. I was worried about:

- My family and friends not accepting my lifestyle changes.
- Being ridiculed for being 'cracked'.
- People around town treating me like a leper or 'broken'.
- Slipping back into my old habits and ways.
- Slipping back into depression.
- Going back to work.

But you know what? One day at a time, minute by minute, everything has turned out just fine. I had a different way of looking at life, and a new set of tools to deal with things.

The most important thing is to keep working on your Basix—it is a lifelong commitment to yourself. It requires constant work and resources to keep up to scratch, it is not easy, but it is worth it. You are worth it!

When you get the Basix right, and you follow your heart and your fear, life mysteriously takes off—you end up in a state of 'flow'.

I believe that everything happens for a reason, and that everything in my life to date happened so that I could learn, grow and share what I have learned with you: My childhood, school years, the bouts of depression, the many sliding doors moments, the desperation, the commitment to change, the help, the learning and the hard work.

That all led to a pivotal point where Margret sent me a link to '30 Days of Genius' which featured James Altucher, who wrote *Choose Yourself!*, advocating '10 ideas daily practice', which gave me the idea to write this book.

Life is:
- A roller coaster: up, down, fun, scary, exciting, boring … repeat.
- Failing and trying again.
- Learning and growth.
- Loving and losing.
- Giving and receiving.
- Acceptance and compassion.

Make better decisions backed by 100% commitment, put habits in place to reach your goals, address your beliefs, fuel your body correctly, exercise, all with peace of mind and you are halfway there. Get the Basix right, hold yourself to a higher standard and magic happens.

It has been a long journey for myself to get to this point. It has not been cheap, or easy. The information in this book has worked for me and is still working for me. Sometimes I falter, but I just get back up, dust myself off, and make it happen once again. I feel great and I look better every day. Life is treating me well, and I am very happy. I am OK with all of my past and I am thinking clearly, and most importantly, I have better ideas.

Will all of this work for you? That is entirely up to YOU, as YOU have the choice to sit on the sideline or get in the game of life. It is up to YOU to make it happen for YOU, so do yourself a favour and give it a good hard crack! YOU won't regret it. Feel the fear of change and lean into it, use it as a guide and go for it! And most importantly, DO it for yourself.

Let me leave you with another quote from one of my favourite movies:

> *"Your future is whatever you make it, so make it a good one!"*
> Dr Emmet Brown, Back to the Future 3

Feedback

Thank you for reading DeFunkMe: The Basix. I sincerely hope you have found real value in this book.

I need your help! Please take a minute to rate this book and leave a brief but honest review, wherever you purchased it. It is only a small thing, but reviews make a big difference to authors and our success.

I would love to hear any of your feedback, thoughts, and stories of change in your life. Please also share with me what you took away from this book, what you found useful or any sections that you just couldn't stomach. Email ANY feedback through to me at ian@defunkme.com . I may not always be able to respond to your emails but I will try my very best!

Visit www.defunkme.com and join our community to keep you up to date with any new information or videos. I will never sell your information to anyone; I hate spam just as much as you do.

Also, join our closed group on facebook, search for 'DeFunkMe Group', where you can actively participate with a community of like-minded people to share information, discuss topics or ask any questions you may have.

I wish you well on your journey.

Much love,

Ian Schell

Palladium Private™

I will be forever grateful to the staff at Palladium Private™ for their help and support for my three-week stay at their retreat in Queensland in November of 2014.

I strongly recommend their services for anyone suffering from stress, depression or anxiety as I found their treatments and services first rate and I now love life again thanks to their help. Their staff are very friendly, compassionate and professional. The quality treatments in such a tranquil setting made the retreat a fantastic experience.

In addition to dealing with stress, depression and anxiety they also offer services for the treatment of drug addiction, alcohol dependency, eating disorders, and post-traumatic stress disorder (PTSD). Their team also includes qualified and experienced psychologists.

For more information go to:
www.palladium-private.com
phone: 1300 198 350 (Aus) or +61 7 5494 2024 (Intl)

I do not receive anything in return for endorsing their services; I just love their work.

P.S. The cost of their services may at first seem expensive, but when you amortise that cost over the rest of your improved life, it becomes negligible. I wish I had known about them years ago. Would I spend that money again for one of my loved ones? Absolutely—in a heartbeat.

Bibliography

Wayne Parrott and Michelle Mark, 2010, *28 Days to Beat the Blues – A practical guide to reducing stress*
Global Publishing Group, Mt Evelyn, Victoria

James Altucher, 2013, *Choose Yourself!*
Lioncrest Publishing

Claudia Azula Altucher, 2015, *Become an Idea Machine – Because ideas are the currency of the 21st century*
Choose Yourself Media LLC

John R Little and Doug McGuff, 2009, *Body By Science*
McGraw-Hill

Chase Jarvis, 2016, *30 Days of Genius*
Creativelive - https://www.creativelive.com/courses/30-days-genius-chase-jarvis

Anthony Robbins, 2014, Post: *Tony Robbins: 6 Basic Needs That Make Us Tick*
Entrepreneur – https://www.entrepreneur.com/article/240441

Further reading

The books mentioned below have been instrumental to my learning. I would re-read any of these. I would strongly recommend all of these to anyone.

Depression and anxiety – *28 Days to Beat the Blues* by Wayne Parrott and Michelle Mark

Fresh thinking – *Choose Yourself!* by James Altucher

Thinking and wealth – *Think and Grow Rich* by Napoleon Hill

Life & Relationships – *Don't Sweat the Small Stuff, and It's All Small Stuff* by Richard Carlson

Spirituality and life – *Conversations with God* by Neale Donald Walsch - 3 book series

Life & Success – *The Magic of Thinking Big* by David Schwartz

Efficiency and relationships – *The 7 Habits of Highly Effective People* by Stephen Covey.

Men's well-being – *Manhood* by Steve Biddulph

Habits – *Better than Before* by Gretchen Rubin

Success & Wealth – *The Millionaire Fastlane* By MJ DeMarco

Efficiency and life design – *The 4-Hour Work Week* by Timothy Ferris

Wealth – *The Choose Yourself Guide To Wealth* by James Altucher

Purpose, business and life – *Unwritten* by Jack Delosa

Business & Entrepreneurship – *Unprofessional* by Jack Delosa

Ideas – *Become An Idea Machine* by Claudia Azula Altucher

Efficiency – *The 80/20 Principle* by Richard Koch

Emotional intelligence – *Emotional intelligence: Why It Can Matter More Than IQ* by Daniel Goleman

Relationships – *How to Win Friends and Influence People* by Dale Carnegie

Relationships – *How to Talk to Anyone* by Leil Lowndes

Management – *The New One Minute Manager* by Ken Blanchard, PHD and Spencer Johnson, MD.

Business & Management – *The Personal MBA* by Josh Kaufman.

Management and change – *Who Moved My Cheese?* by Spencer Johnson, M.D.

Productivity – *Getting Things Done* by David Allen

Kids and communication – *How to Talk So Kids Will Listen and Listen So Kids Will Talk* by Adele Faber and Elaine Mazlish.

Parenting – *The Gifts of Imperfect Parenting* by Brene Brown

Any books by Tony Robbins

About the author

My name is Ian Schell. On my 21st birthday, I tried to take my own life. Obviously, I fucked that up because I'm still here. Again in 2014, I hit rock bottom and had suicidal thoughts. On paper I had it all—a lovely wife, two great kids, a good job with good pay, a renovated house and yet I was severely depressed and suicidal.

With a wife and two kids, suicide wasn't an option and I needed help, badly!

Now, I am the happiest and healthiest I have ever been. When I look back on my crippling depression in 2014, I see it as the best thing that has ever happened to me. Why? Because I finally got the help I needed, and new information and techniques that completely turned my life around. It wasn't easy or cheap, but it was worth it.

My mission is to pass on the information that helped me. My vision is to help others improve their life.

www.ingramcontent.com/pod-product-compliance
Lightning Source LLC
Chambersburg PA
CBHW060929040426
42445CB00011B/854